GENDER TRAUMA

T0271723

by the same author

How to Understand Your Gender
A Practical Guide for Exploring Who You Are
Alex Iantaffi and Meg-John Barker
Foreword by S. Bear Bergman
ISBN 978 1 78592 746 1
eISBN 978 1 78450 517 2

Life Isn't Binary
On Being Both, Beyond, and In-Between
Meg-John Barker and Alex Iantaffi
Foreword by CN Lester
ISBN 978 1 78592 479 8
eISBN 978 1 78450 864 7

of related interest

Cultural Awareness in Therapy with Trans and Gender Non-Conforming Adults and Older People
A Practical Guide
Tavi Hawn, LCSW
ISBN 978 1 78592 838 3
eISBN 978 1 78592 2664 8

Person-Centred Counselling for Trans and Gender Diverse People
A Practical Guide
Sam Hope
ISBN 978 1 78592 542 9
eISBN 978 1 78450 937 8

Working with Trans Survivors of Sexual Violence
A Guide for Professionals
Sally Rymer and Valentina Cartei
ISBN 978 1 78592 760 7
eISBN 978 1 78450 618 6

Gender Trauma

Healing Cultural, Social, and
Historical Gendered Trauma

Alex Iantaffi

Foreword by Meg-John Barker

Jessica Kingsley Publishers
London and Philadelphia

First published in Great Britain in 2021 by Jessica Kingsley Publishers
An Hachette Company

3

Copyright © Alex Iantaffi 2021
Foreword copyright © Meg-John Barker 2021

A CIP catalogue record for this title is available from the British
Library and the Library of Congress

ISBN 978 1 78775 106 4
eISBN 978 1 78775 107 1

Printed and bound by CPI Group (UK) Ltd, Croydon, CR0 4YY

Jessica Kingsley Publishers' policy is to use papers that are natural,
renewable and recyclable products and made from wood grown
in sustainable forests. The logging and manufacturing processes
are expected to conform to the environmental regulations of the
country of origin.

Jessica Kingsley Publishers
73 Collier Street
London N1 9BE, UK

www.jkp.com

*This book is dedicated to Indigenous resistors everywhere,
and all the ancestors who made this possible.*

Contents

Foreword

There are people in your life who act as lighthouses. Alex Iantaffi has been one of those people for me, and for many, many others I suspect. Time after time I've been adrift in stormy seas, at risk of being cast upon the jagged rocks. Alex's wisdom has been a guiding light for me through those times, although it has often taken me a while to follow it.

- They came to an understanding of their trans and nonbinary gender. Some time later, I found my way to mine.
- I heard them speak about family systems, about complex PTSD and the body, and about their role in damaging relationship dynamics. Years on I was finally able to see the deep traces of all those things through my own life.
- They introduced me to the idea of gender as a form of cultural, intergenerational, and historical trauma, interwoven with all other forms of colonization, dehumanization, and oppression. Something clicked, and now—as I sit and write this during the early months of

the global pandemic—I see so clearly the many ways in which gender oppression has wounded me, has operated through me to hurt others, and is inseparable from the damage that humans have wrought upon each other and upon the planet.

I suspect that, for many of us, this moment of global trauma brings more personal traumas to life again. As our nervous systems activate to the potential threat we are reminded of the times when our bodies have felt like this in the past: the out-of-control adrenaline of fight and flight, the terrifying immobility of freeze and fawn.

At this moment I feel deeply connected to my female socialization: to the ways in which I was taught to be for others, never for myself; to appease and placate in the face of potential threat or violence. I see the cultural and intergenerational gaslighting that taught me to deny and minimize any painful or violating experiences, to blame myself for these and to defend those hurting me, to internalize the knowledge that my freedom and safety was less important than another person's—even mild—discomfort. I'm aware of how this set me—and my sisters—up for experiences of sexual assault, of controlling relationships, of workplace bullying, and of seeing our bodies and understandings as inevitably less important than those of others, constantly doubting and criticizing ourselves

The #MeToo movement is just the tip of the iceberg of the conversation which needs to happen now. We all need to address our complicity in these gendered dynamics which have damaged all of us caught up in them. We also need to acknowledge how gender intersects with so many other axes of oppression to determine whose stories even get told and heard. I keep returning to the everyday horror of how brief those moments are when a person places themselves in the role of perpetrator, and another in the role of survivor, irrevocably, and how the utterly non-consensual world we all grew up in sets us all up for such moments. It's hard to bear.

As a trans person at this moment I also feel the weight of the past few years of trans moral panic. The pandemic lands as an uneasy relief from finding ourselves attacked day after day in the media. Finally they have something else to talk about. At the same time, trans people are coming to this global trauma on the heels of an elongated period of trauma which involved witnessing our legitimacy—our very existence—being called into question on a daily basis: by the experts, practitioners, and gatekeepers who denied us agency and bodily autonomy, and by the families, friends, and colleagues whose accurate mirroring of our lived experience would have been so vital to our wellbeing and sense of self. We're emerging from the everyday cultural gaslighting of being labelled abusive perpetrators when we know how many of us—particularly trans feminine people of color—lose their lives every day, and how many of us are assaulted, discriminated against, and worn down by a hundred daily papercuts of microaggressions and misgendering.

I have advocated hard for this book ever since Alex mentioned it to me. Therapists and other practitioners are rarely—if ever—trained on:

- gender and how it intersects with all other axes of oppression
- the cultural, structural, and systemic context in which their clients' struggles occur
- the ways in which trauma operates through our external

and internal systems, becoming locked in our bodies and brains, and how this can be addressed.

Drawing on their expertise in systemic therapy and somatic experiencing, their scholarship in queer and intersectional feminism, and their decades of experience working clinically with individuals and families of all genders, Alex clearly explains—through this book—how the current rigid, binary, essentialist system of gender harms us all: how it is—in itself—a form of trauma. They locate this in the legacy of settler colonialism and historical trauma, explaining how it is passed on through families and communities in the form of intergenerational trauma.

Through thoughtful moments, educational stretches, and clinical vignettes, Alex helps us as readers to reflect on our own location in relation to gender trauma, to understand how it applies to our everyday lives, and to learn how those of us who are clinicians or practitioners might work with those most affected to alleviate suffering, rather than exacerbating it and reinforcing gender trauma as our professions so often have in the past.

This book is so desperately needed that I had already referenced it—long prior to publication—in several of my own books. Every person I've mentioned it to has been desperate to get their hands on a copy. I am so glad that it will finally be out in the world sharing the vital wisdoms and experiences that Alex has woven together so beautifully.

Like Alex themself, this book is a lighthouse. A lighthouse shines through the darkness, turmoil, and confusion of the storm. It never insists that you follow it. But when you do—when you eventually feel ready to trust that light—you can finally reach a safe-enough harbour.

Meg-John Barker co-author of *How to Understand Your Gender* and *Life Isn't Binary*

Acknowledgements

I am grateful to the traditional custodians of the lands on which I was raised, on which I currently live, and where I have written this book. I am particularly grateful to all the Indigenous elders, scholars, activists and resistors for their ongoing work, every day. I am thankful for all the scholars, community organizers, authors, activists, mentioned and unmentioned in this book, who have engaged with gender and without whom this work would not have been possible. I am grateful to all ancestors who have resisted rigid gender binaries across space and time, and also made this work possible. Finally, I am grateful to my family: I could not do any of this without your love and practical support. Thank you.

Introduction

Who am I?

I have been intrigued and puzzled by gender for as long as I can remember. This book is, in part, the result of 49 years of puzzlement. During this time, I managed to get a whole PhD studying gender and disability in education. I studied child development, both as part of my training as an elementary school teacher in Italy in my late teens and early 20s, and as part of my training as a family therapist in my very early 30s in the UK. I taught what used to be called "Women's Studies." I read feminist manifestos and neurobiology-focused books on gender and brain development. I researched many aspects of gender, as well as sexuality and relationships. I came to understand my own gender better, and came out as trans masculine and nonbinary. I experience being displaced, partially due to my gender and sexuality, from the places where I was born and brought up, and I keep asking myself questions such as: "What am I doing here?" and "How do we collectively heal?". Alongside many other brilliant people, I advocated for gender liberation for everyone and continue to do so. I sat with people of all genders for thousands and thousands of hours as a therapist. I educated thousands of people about gender through public speaking and training. I talked about—and deconstructed—gender with my children, my partners, family, friends and colleagues. As I write this, I am aware that how much I thought about gender might seem a tad obsessive! However, as an academic at heart, despite leaving the academy, I am well aware of how some of us become fascinated by certain aspects of life, and then dedicate much of our lives to understanding these aspects better. So, this book comes from all that.

Why this book and who is it for?

Writing this book was terrifying, and sending it out into the world is too. I wanted this book to exist, yet I felt inadequate to the task of such an enterprise. Am I the right person to write this book? How can I go to the heart of gender essentialism, lay bare its origin, history, and structures, and how they impact us still? This is what I am trying to do in this book. I am trying to show how all of us—people of all genders—are impacted, and how few of us—if any—benefit from a rigid, binary system of gender. I also want this book to contain useful ideas about how to work with all of this, especially in therapeutic and educational contexts. This is why you will find thoughtful moments, educational stretches and clinical vignettes throughout this book. All clinical vignettes are composite from a range of experiences and cases in order to protect confidentiality. They come from the entirety of my clinical and supervisory experiences so far, as well as from my teaching and community organizing. I believe this book can be helpful to all healthcare providers, as well as to educators and activists. I am also hoping that this book might be accessible enough for an educated general reader who may want more, after reading one of my previous books, *How to Understand Your Gender*, co-authored with Meg-John Barker. You can begin to comprehend that this is indeed an ambitious enterprise! I hope that this book becomes just a piece of a larger, much needed dialogue.

What is the story through this book?

Starting from the idea that the pervasiveness of the gender binary is part of the legacy of settler colonialism, and therefore a historical trauma, I proceed to unpack how this still impacts us in a range of ways depending on our geographical, social, economic and cultural locations. From the current landscape, I then move on to a closer look at how gender is also passed on from generation to generation within families before looking at how gender plays out in a range of relationships. I spend a little time focusing on systems, such as the law, education, healthcare and so on. I finally draw some conclusions on the importance of healing gendered trauma for future generations, as well as for ourselves.

Throughout the book I do my best to address gender, not only as an isolated construct, but as a facet of our lives that intersects with many other aspects of our identities, histories and experiences, such as Indigeneity, race and ethnicity, class, disability, religion and so on. At the end of each chapter there is a summary of the main points made.

I also want to make it clear that, although I have pulled the story together in this specific way, I am drawing from a vast body of knowledge, including Indigenous scholars and activists, and Black and Latinx scholars and organizers, especially feminist ones. Any mistakes, misinterpretations and blunders remain my own though. However, this book would not have been possible without the work of these scholars and activists. I am also aware of my own position as an Italian-raised immigrant benefitting from white privilege, disabled, trans masculine, nonbinary, queer person. While identity labels can only tell a very small part of the story, I feel it is still important to name some of those aspects to better position myself for you, the readers. By choosing to write this book, I am also choosing to be accountable for its content, especially to communities who are most impacted by the ongoing, settler colonial gendered violence, such as Indigenous women and LGBTQ2 people and trans feminine people of color. If I have missed something, moved out of my lane or misspoken, I am truly sorry.

How to read this book

The book is meant to be read in a linear fashion. However, we all have different ways of learning. Please feel free to pick a chapter that interests you if that feels more accessible or useful to you. Bear in mind, though, that some concepts might have been introduced earlier in the book.

I hope this book is helpful to you in some way, whether you are a therapist, educator, community organizer or provider of some kind, or just someone who is intrigued and puzzled by gender. You will likely not agree with everything I have written, and that is a good thing! As written extensively in another of my previous books, *Life Isn't Binary*, also co-authored with Meg-John Barker, I firmly believe in the necessity of a plurality of views. Ultimately my hope is that this book honors the ancestors, opens a path for any descendants, and contributes to the ongoing dialogues about gender and its role in our lives.

Given one of the subjects of this book, trauma, this book is full of triggers. I address several aspects of gendered violence, including settler colonial violence, racialized aspects of violence, transphobia and transmisogyny, and more. I am aware that certain parts of the book will impact different bodies in very specific ways. I know I personally had a hard time writing this book. I had to take several breaks. I was three months late on the originally agreed deadline. It is one of the hardest books I have written to date, and I believe it might be an emotionally challenging book to read. Please take care as you read this book. I have not inserted "slow down pages" in this book, as in previous ones, because I felt I would have needed them after each subsection at least. I still invite you to take time to pause and notice how you are doing as you read. Is your body tense? Are you feeling light-headed, or numb? As and when you notice a significant shift in your sensations, emotions or thoughts, please stop and take care of yourself. The book will still be there when you are ready to pick it up again. Reading it with others is another option, especially with others you trust, so you can support one another. If you are using this book as an educational tool, such as a textbook, please consider how to best support the learners with whom you do this work. Thank you.

CHAPTER 1

How did we get here?

It is easy to romanticize the past and imagine there was an ideal historical moment when gender was completely liberated from any societal constraints. This is not what I am trying to do here. The goal of this first chapter is to set the scene. I firmly believe that we cannot understand the present and imagine the potentiality of the future without understanding the past. It would be beyond the scope of this book to provide a comprehensive historical perspective on the topic of gender. What I attempt instead is to challenge the idea that a rigid gender binary has always existed, discuss how Indigenous perspectives are an essential part of this conversation, why settler colonialism, the patriarchy and gender essentialism are tightly woven together, how some science has perpetuated the myth of a rigid gender binary as natural and foundational, and how some contemporary feminist science is challenging that same myth. In this chapter I also introduce the idea of a rigid gender binary as an aspect of historical trauma and provide some suggestions for how to begin working with this idea.

1.1 Gender and the ongoing settler colonial project

Let's start by defining some terms that will be used throughout the book. Gender is certainly one of the first terms to define given that it's in the title of the book. Gender is a large biopsychosocial construct, which includes aspects of identity, expression, role and experience, as addressed in one of my previous books, *How to Understand Your Gender* (Iantaffi and Barker 2018).

"Biopsychosocial" means that gender can be viewed as a mix of biological traits (and by this I include things like our chromosomal composition and our brains), psychological characteristics and social interactions. I'll address later why reducing gender to being synonymous with what some people call biological sex is reductive and inadequate. For now, when I write "gender" I mean a complex construct that might include some or all of these facets. I use additional qualifiers, such as identity, expression, role, experience and so on if I refer to these particular aspects of gender.

In dominant Western paradigms it is assumed either that gender is separate from biology and completely social and cultural, or that it is inevitably linked to external physical characteristics, such as our genitals and secondary sex characteristics. If this seems contradictory, it's because it is! As you can imagine much confusion can arise from this. In everyday discourse, we also have a common understanding of what gender means. For example, if someone said they wanted to know the gender of the baby when someone was pregnant, we would assume that they would want to know what genitals the baby had based on current imaging technology. The underlying assumption is that genitals define what sex and gender will be assigned to this child at birth legally, culturally and socially. Usually, unless people are immersed in—or deeply engaged with—trans and/or nonbinary communities, this means they're referring to two possibilities: boy/girl, male/female. This ideology has been called cisgenderism by some scholars. It is the idea that there are two genders—male and female—clearly identifiable by genitals and sex characteristics, and that this system is based on science and fact, and therefore natural. This ideology is often assumed to be universal: that is, true across time and space. However what gender means varies across both time and space: in other words, across history and geography.

This leads me to defining settler colonialism, the other term used in the title of this section, given that I start from looking at the rigidity of the gender binary as an aspect of historical trauma. Settler colonialism is a specific type of colonialism. In this model of colonialism, the settlers' goal is to create structures that over time allow them to replace the Indigenous populations previously inhabiting the same space. Settler colonialism doesn't just happen at one point in history; it is an ongoing project that continuously undermines Indigenous identities, culture and sovereignty.

For example, in the place we currently call the United States, the containment, erasure and harm to Indigenous Native American communities is ongoing and enacted through legislative, educational, military and social structures. The project of the United States as a settler colonial state was not over once the colonial rule of the British government was overthrown, but rather it continued in the creation and maintenance of a sovereign settler state. Some settler colonial studies also highlight how settler colonialism impacts global politics so that we live, in the words of Lorenzo Veracini (2015), "in a settler colonial global present."

Another example of the ongoing settler colonial present on a global level is the erasure of the Sami people, Indigenous to northern Scandinavia, in places like Norway, Sweden and Finland. It is only in recent years, and due to global Indigenous organizing, that the Sami people have been recognized by these settler colonial states as Indigenous. The impact of genocide, erasure, and cultural and linguistic destruction though are still felt in Sami communities. Many Sami people migrated and have hidden their identities for survival, at times assimilating into whiteness in other settler colonial states, such as Canada and the United States. This and the active prosecution of cultural practices, such as yoiking—a traditional style of Sami singing or chanting—have led to the disintegration of many Sami communities.

There are many more examples globally of settler colonialism, and how its impact is current and ongoing. I invite you to check out the further reading at the end of the book if you are interested in knowing more about settler colonialism. For now, you may be asking yourself, why talk about settler colonialism in a book on gender? It seems time to bring it all together.

Our current understanding of gender is deeply impacted by settler colonial practices. Many Indigenous cultures, in fact, have more than two words to refer to gender. Gender itself seemed to historically be, in many Indigenous cultures, a concept more connected with identity, expression and role than biology. Staying with the example of what we currently know as the United States and Canada, several tribal nations had multiple words to refer to gender and have always had people who did not fall into a rigid gender binary. The latter was not historically seen as pathological or abnormal in any way, but rather as part of human expression, which is why words and roles existed to indicate the expansiveness of gender. However, when European settlers invaded the Americas, they did not know how to understand this gender expansiveness. Their lack of understanding was, in turn, a product of imperialism and Christianization, which had already effectively erased and driven gender expansiveness underground across Europe.

These settlers referred to Indigenous people whose gender did not make sense to them as berdache, a term that is considered offensive in Native communities. For these settlers, this was but another example of how Indigenous people were, in their view, "savage" and as such less than human. The narrative of the Indigenous people as savages in need of taming and educating served the structures of settler colonialism. If Indigenous people could be considered as less than human as non-Christians, then their land could be taken, and they could be enslaved and/or forcibly assimilated into the new settler colonial state. The gender expansiveness of many tribal nations was yet another challenge to Christian, patriarchal hegemony.

Gender expansiveness was not the only challenge to settler colonial ideology. Issues like more egalitarian gender roles, matrilineal traditions and adoption were also seen as undesirable by settlers. To this day, in the United States, the question of who can be enrolled in a tribal nation is a challenging one and tribes might have different criteria than those used by the government. Controlling bodies, gender, relationships, language, culture and spirituality is an essential element of settler colonial states. Therefore, it is impossible to talk about the impact of a rigid gender binary without acknowledging that settler colonialism, and the enforced Christianization that usually accompanies it, played and still play crucial roles in perpetuating this dichotomy.

For many of us it might be impossible to conceive of a

construct of gender that is not linked to biology given that even historical accounts are often based on looking at the past through the lenses of the present. For example, most historical documentaries look at gender in a binary, biology-driven way. Let's use the Vikings as an example of this. Most written accounts of Norse (Viking) cultures were created post-Christianity and assign different societal roles to men and women. However, it only takes looking at this culture a little more closely and in depth to hypothesize that societal structures were far more driven by roles such as warrior, farmer, spiritual authority or clan leader than gender, given that people of all genders could be found in these roles. Post-Christian interpretations of history have permeated the collective imagination through books, movies, documentaries and poetry to the point that we have needed to actively re-imagine and re-member people outside of a cisgender binary of male/female back into a history of which they were already part. Erasure is but one facet of the ripples of history. As someone who is partially displaced because of gender and sexuality, I feel the ripples across history and geography that led me, and many others, halfway across the globe, far too often inflicting the same violence that had been inflicted upon our ancestors. These are the ripples of intergenerational and ongoing settler colonial violence. This is why I have come to realize that we cannot talk about gender without talking about Indigeneity, the impact of settler colonial practices and of Christianization. In what we now call the United States, the ripples and waves of violence were given the name of historical trauma.

Historical trauma is a term used to indicate the cumulative impact of historical events that affected people from one generation to the next. As far as I am aware, the term historical trauma was first coined and used in the 1980s by Indigenous scholar Dr. Maria Yellow Horse Brave Heart (Hunkpapa/Oglala Lakota) who compared the impact of the Holocaust on survivors with that of events like the Wounded Knee massacre on the Lakota people. It was her scholarship that hypothesized that a range of disparate actions and events can have similar impacts on different populations and can, as such, be grouped under the umbrella term of historical trauma. Impact of historical trauma can manifest as higher rates of depression, anxiety, substance use, alcoholism, suicide, intimate partner violence and abuse. Her scholarship clearly indicated that those issues, which are often seen as individualized mental health or domestic issues, are indeed symptoms of horrific collective trauma and unresolved grief. This idea has challenged, and continues to challenge, the fields of psychology, mental health and public health. She also discussed how the current political and social climate continues to exacerbate the impact of this ongoing genocide on Indigenous populations. Although I refer to her work and consider it foundational, any missteps in my interpretation and use in this book are my own. I strongly invite you to read and cite her scholarship directly.

For the purposes of this book, what do I mean when I say that a rigid gender binary is an aspect of historical trauma steeped in the ongoing settler colonial project?

As stated earlier, part of Christianization and settler colonialism has been the erasure of gender expansive identities, roles, expressions and experiences. This has meant loss of language and terminology for people who do not fall into a rigid binary, which has also meant the erasure and dislocation of what we now might call queer, intersex, nonbinary and transgender people. In fact the term Two-Spirit was invented as an English-based term by a coalition of Indigenous people from a range of tribal nations to reclaim what was lost and create space for their legitimacy and existence. However, not all Indigenous people use, or relate to, this term. The impact of the historical erasure of gender expansive people though is not only felt by people who we might now call queer, intersex, nonbinary and transgender. While queer, intersex, nonbinary and trans people are impacted in specific ways by this aspect of historical trauma, I posit that people of all genders are impacted as well, and that in order for us to move towards authentic gender liberation, we need to recognize and reckon with this impact. We also need to make sure not to conflate the distinct ways in which we are impacted into a singular form of oppression. For example, although displaced from my own relationship with land, language, culture and ancestors in Sicily, I also benefit from white supremacy as an immigrant and new settler, both because of having a lighter skin colour and because of the assimilation of Italian identities into whiteness in what is currently known as the US. I will ask you readers to hold complexity throughout the book, to not resort to an easy rhetoric in which we're all impacted in similar ways, because we are not, and to recognize those who are most impacted in our communities.

Thoughtful moment: what did you learn in history about gender?

For now, take a moment to breathe. You might notice all sorts of emotions, sensations and thoughts rising up as you read this weaving of history through the lens of gender. I invite you to take a moment to reflect on how all this information is landing for you, recognizing that this will be impacted by your own location in relationship to history. Think back to what you have learned about history, in relation to gender, when and where you grew up.

Whose history was taught and from which perspective? How was gender depicted in textbooks and narratives used to teach such history? Was your learning as a child challenged by information you acquired later on? If so, how? What was the new information you acquired and where did it come from? How does what you learned still impact the way you look at gender now, both within yourself and in others? Have you read anything in this chapter so far that challenges your understanding of gender? If so, what? It might be that these ideas are already very familiar to you. If so, read on. If not, it's ok to take a moment to digest these ideas through discussion with colleagues, journaling or just sitting with this information. Of course, you can always read on and come back to reflect further at a later time.

1.2 The rise of gender essentialism

I stated in the previous section that "controlling bodies, gender, relationships, language, culture and spirituality is an essential element of settler colonial states." Let's take a moment to break this down further. If the goal of settlers is to replace Indigenous populations with themselves, then controlling reproduction and bodies is an important part of this process. In many ways some of the initial colonizers who first came to settle on a different land had been controlled themselves. For example, the British government would often send felons to their colonies. Others were escaping religious persecution. Many colonizers, unless they were privileged upper class or noble cis men, had already been othered before becoming settlers. As it often happens with trauma, we tend to enact what we know, what is familiar. It is not very surprising then that settlers would often attempt to control both one another and Native people through the same violent, assimilatory tools that had been used against them. Black, Brown and Indigenous bodies had already been constructed, within the Western dominant imaginary, as other and less than human so that they could be controlled, enslaved, assimilated and deprived of autonomy and sovereignty.

This pattern was perpetuated through the promulgation of the "Doctrine of Discovery," around the middle of the 15th century onwards. The doctrine allowed Christian Europeans to take possession of any land not under the ruling of a Christian European monarch. The premise underlying the Doctrine of Discovery was that only Christian European men (and it was just men) could be considered legitimate citizens and, as such, fully human. The impact of the Doctrine of Discovery on Indigenous populations was still a matter of discussions in fora such as the United Nations (UN) as recently as 2012, even though the UN had already adopted the Declaration on the Rights of Indigenous People in 2007.

It is no coincidence that around the time that the Doctrine of Discovery was used to justify the expansion of settler colonial empires and monarchies, the persecution, trial and killing of witches was also taking hold in many parts of Europe. This was happening especially in regions governed by the same monarchs who were also promulgating the Doctrine of Discovery. Witches were usually healers and midwives who had knowledge considered dangerous by the ruling classes, such as how to prevent and terminate pregnancies. Bodies capable of reproduction are also bodies that are seen as out of the control of external governance.

The historical tight control of sexuality, especially for people assigned female at birth and for queer people, is also linked to this need for governance of bodies that is essential to the settler colonial project. Only when we other the land can we own the soil and the green and red bloods—that is, plants and animals, including human animals—that are sustained by it. Only when we other bodies can we own, control and govern them. Any bodies that were not under rule of a Christian cis white male, whether land or people, were in some ways seen as ungovernable and, as such, both threatening and desirable. You can start to see how much of settler colonialism is framed by beliefs that justify and promote control and ownership. Once more though, what does this have to do with gender?

In many ways people who fall outside of cisnormativity and heteronormativity—that is, the assumption that people's gender identity is aligned with their sex assigned at birth, and that they will "naturally" be attracted to people of the "opposite" gender—have always been the most challenging to settler colonial states. First of all, they did not fit into the Christian paradigm, which had adopted ideas from Greek philosophers like Aristotle, in which there were two sexes, male and female, with women being seen as subject to the rule of men. Therefore not only were people who fell outside this Christian binary of male/female considered a threat, but also any system that was either egalitarian, not strictly and biologically binary based, or matriarchal was also a threat to these views on which the rest of the settler colonial project was being built.

This might all seem like ancient history in some ways, yet as I write this in 2019 on Turtle Island, currently known as the United States, several states are facing legislation proposals that would ban or severely restrict abortions. As journalist Michael

Harriot pointed out in an article in *The Root* (2019), in Georgia and Alabama 211 out of the 212 lawmakers who voted in favor of these legislative changes to ban or restrict abortions were white. As they point out this does not necessarily reflect the beliefs of the general population, which according to research is mostly in favor of people's sovereignty over their bodies and reproduction. This reflects a political situation, which is about racialized dynamics within party politics in the current US system. The Republican party has historically placed itself as the party of white people, and so whether people may or may not agree with the issue of who can control reproduction, they will fall in line with the identity they have been told to hang on to the tightest: whiteness, a fragile yet powerful category at the heart of the settler colonial project as we are examining in this chapter.

Whiteness can, in fact, not be separated from the need to control gender in rigid ways. We could also say that we cannot talk of gender without talking about how bodies are racialized. Staying with the example of reproductive rights on Turtle Island—that is, the current United States—many cis white women felt the depiction of women's fertility being controlled by a totalitarian government in *The Handmaid's Tale*, a TV show based on Margaret Atwood's novel (1985/1996), was "too close to current reality." However, these comments failed to acknowledge the historical fact that the bodies of Indigenous, Black and Brown women have already been treated this way, not only while slavery was still legal in the US, and when residential schools would take Indigenous children away from their families and communities, but also with current border control practices, in which very young children are separated from their parents, and at times given to white families to foster or adopt. We can never talk about gender as if it was devoid of both racialized and colonial dynamics.

I suggest then that the roots of gender essentialism can indeed be traced back not just to some Greek philosophers, but more actively to the period between the end of the middle ages and the beginning of the modern era, a period in which many sought to control bodies for exploitation and colonial dominance. What is gender essentialism though and how is it different from the ideology of cisgenderism, already introduced in the previous section? Gender essentialism is the idea that there are certain innate qualities to being male and female. In some ways cisgenderism is the foundation on which gender essentialism is built. Cisgenderism is the ideology that tells us that it is "natural" to only have two sexes and for gender to be aligned with one's sex assigned at birth. Within cisgenderism, trans, nonbinary and gender expansive identities might be tolerated within a framework of pathology. Gender essentialism is the ideology that tells us that men and women have certain characteristics that are inherent to their sex assigned at birth, on which gender is also defined. In many ways gender essentialism conflates sex and gender in one. In this ideology, for example, women tend to be viewed as naturally more nurturing and caring, whereas men as usually more aggressive and competitive.

Both cisgenderism and gender essentialism are the building blocks of the patriarchy. Cisgenderism is needed to ensure that a cis binary gender is viewed as naturally occurring, and gender essentialism is needed to theorize women's subordination to men as somehow also natural and scientific. Gender essentialism has been on the rise, as stated earlier, since the 15th century and, in many ways, it has not yet let go of its hold on dominant culture. Misogyny and what has more recently been called "rape culture" are both underlined by gender essentialism. I address this further in Chapter 4, when I discuss relationships.

Feminism, especially since the 1700s onward has been challenging the notion of gender essentialism from Mary Wollstonecraft's *A Vindication of the Rights of Woman* (1792/2020) to Sojourner Truth's abolitionist and women's rights campaigning. These efforts continued through the writing of Simone de Beauvoir, bell hooks, Angela Davis, Audre Lorde and Judith Butler, to name but a few. Much of these efforts highlight how gender is socially and culturally constructed and often has, at the heart, the goal of equality between genders, albeit often still subscribing to the idea of only two genders.

In the next chapter I address more specifically how feminism also struggles with the legacy of gender essentialism and the ongoing legacy of a colonial cisgenderist binary concept of gender. For now, we will pause here and look at why all of this might be relevant to your practice as a clinician, before proceeding to address how science has been both complicit in reinforcing gender essentialism and, more recently, active in challenging it across disciplines ranging from gender studies to queer theory to neuroscience.

▼ Clinical vignette: gender essentialism in sex therapy

At this point, you might think that gender essentialism only lives on in TV shows like *Mad Men*, depicting a past where men were men and women were women, whatever that meant at the time. You might be surprised how often gender essentialism might be showing up in the therapy room. Here it's a common scenario that many of you working with couples might recognize.

"Tom and Anna have been married for 25 years. They met in college and have been together ever since. Their child has recently left home and they consider themselves empty nesters. Both have careers they love, friends they have known for a long time and are generally happy with their lives. However, they are concerned about their marriage. They have not had sex in several years due to Anna struggling with pain during intercourse. Anna doesn't care if it hurts and regrets telling Tom, after several years, that intercourse was painful for her. Tom is not willing to intentionally cause pain to Anna in this way. Anna is often angry with Tom and feels he no longer finds her attractive despite his reassurance to the contrary. Anna's gynecologist has found no physical reason for the pain so referred her and Tom to a sex therapist."

If you are a sex therapist you might already be thinking of several interventions after reading this. For example, you might encourage Tom and Anna to broaden their sexual intimacy beyond intercourse by introducing techniques such as sensate focus. You might explore whether there is a traumatic incident in Anna's life that has led to the pain she experiences. All these, and other more traditional sex therapy techniques, can be incredibly valuable and effective. However, they might not address some of the underlying issues that Tom and Anna are facing.

For example, Anna has received a message from dominant culture that her erotic capital as a cis straight woman is dependent on male gaze and desire. She has also received a message that men are supposed to be sexually aggressive and dominant. Tom's reluctance to hurt her is not seen as care by Anna but rather as sexual lack of interest. She is feeling anxious about having sex as she is afraid that Tom will eventually leave her if they continue down this road. Tom has also received similar messages but his experience feels at odds with what he has been told. He does not find the idea of hurting someone he loves a turn on, even though he is still attracted to Anna. He feels frustrated and helpless but doesn't have the tools to express these feelings because having emotional conversations has not been a skill that was nurtured for him either in his family of origin or through his schooling. Tom has become more and more depressed and often stays out late drinking with friends after work.

More transformative clinical interventions can gently invite the clients into a noticing, identifying and questioning of gendered messaging they both received so that they can see how they impact their relationship and sexual intimacy. Tom and Anna can then choose whether they want to intentionally keep believing those messages or challenge them in their own lives through the creation of new relational and sexual scripts. As therapists we have the option to offer a reframe where gender essentialism is made visible so that clients can engage with it in a more conscious and intentional way, rather than experiencing it as a force that is silently and covertly shaping their lives and their most intimate relationships.

Take a moment to reflect on how you would approach these clients. What other aspects of their identities, roles and experiences might be important to know? Would this scenario play differently if some of these aspects were changed?

1.3 The role of science

We started this chapter by highlighting how gender has historically been more expansive than it is currently considered to be in Western dominant culture, and how settler colonialism played a major part in restricting gender identities, expressions and roles. Ideologies, such as the Doctrine of Discovery discussed above, were instrumental in this process as was science, across a range of disciplines.

It is to the role of various scientific disciplines in both upholding and more recently challenging gender essentialism that we turn now. For example, the idea of gender essentialism itself rests on the larger concept of biological determinism. Biological determinism is the belief that our behaviors are connected to specific biological traits, such as genetics, physiology and so on. Biological determinism is connected not only with the idea that there are biological differences between the sexes but also with scientific racism and eugenics. If these all seem like ideas from the past, it is enough to look at the popularity of books such as *Men Are from Mars, Women Are from Venus* by John Gray (1992), which has sold more than 15 million copies, the common practice of gender reveal parties, and the prevalence of gender stereotypes in many popular TV shows like *The Big Bang Theory*, *Two and a Half Men* and *Game of Thrones*. Biological determinism still seems to have a strong appeal when it comes to perceived differences between "two sexes" and it is so entrenched in popular culture that we take it just like the air we breathe in. In some ways being exposed to it is unavoidable.

This means that biological determinism not only influences popular self-help writing books, like the one mentioned in the above paragraph, but also academic science and research. Much research in psychology, for example, is still looking at gender differences in a binary way. For example, when I asked to clarify why a research project on dating did not include people of all genders, a researcher at a conference a few years ago replied that they needed a "baseline" first. The implication was that the baseline is considered to be, in much of science, cisgender, that is having a gender identity aligned with the sex assigned at birth, binary (male/female), and mostly white and young as was indeed the case in this project. Who is considered to be the baseline population in science then is heavily dependent on who is seen as having legitimacy as subjects—not just objects—of research. These, in Anglo paradigms, are usually cisgender white, often but no longer exclusively straight, people. In some ways the feminist project has seen the inclusion of cis white women alongside cis white men but not the dismantling of the underlying ideology.

Psychology is but an example. Similar points can be made for sociology, and clinical and public health research. Most research trials do not have an option for my gender or do not give me the opportunity to indicate my sex assigned at birth as different from my gender when relevant. Most public health data can tell us information about the difference between (cis) men and women, sometimes broken down by other aspects of identity such as race and ethnicity, but not others such as disability or class. Much of science views gender as a potential key difference, yet most research studies fail to justify why this is the case and whether the major difference is about identity, role, expression or biology, unless the focus of the research is gender outside of a strict binary. This practice persists as customary despite the fact that, often, there are far fewer differences between genders than, for example, between different cultures or socioeconomic classes.

More often than not researchers, when looking at gender differences, are focusing on biological aspects such as hormone levels, brain composition and other physiological aspects. Sociologists and other social scientists might be focusing instead on differences between gender roles, identities, expressions and experiences. However, they are also often bound by a dichotomous gender binary, dictated by physiology and social, legal, educational and cultural structures. This has led to generation after generation of scientists being brought up within similar paradigms, unless they are located within certain institutions or mentored by specific scientists who are challenging this ideology. The ideal research subjects remain the ideal settler colonial body: that is, European, preferably Anglo or assimilated into whiteness, cisgender, straight, abled and educated. There are, of course, exceptions but that is exactly what they are and, as such, reinforce the fact that there is a norm.

Neuroscience is one of the most recent disciplines to the conversation. Some scientists have turned to neuroscience to prove that there are indeed differences between male and female brains. Researchers looking at transgender identities have also turned to this discipline to prove the legitimacy of these identities. For example, some research has shown that the brains of trans women are more similar to those of cis women than to those of trans men. The search for a biological basis of transgender identities is but another reflection of biological determinism. If it can be proven that we, as trans folks, are indeed "born this way" then our existence can be seen as legitimate and moral. Darwinian evolution has been substituted for creation understandings for many scientists, but it has not necessarily undermined the ideology that only what is considered to be natural and biologically based is valid. If our identities as trans people can be seen as some sort of biological destiny then, and only then, might our existence be seen as part of humanity rather than a distortion of it.

As Sandra Bem illustrated when she said "This is the lens that has secularized God's grand creation by substituting its scientific equivalent: evolution's grand creation" (1993, p.2), moving towards a view where science, instead of God, grants legitimacy to existence, it's really about changing the origination point but not necessarily the knowledge paradigm. In fact, even neuroscience is not immune from the influence of biological determinism. Scientists like Cordelia Fine, who is part of the neurogenderings network, an assortment of scholars from queer and feminist studies with an expertise in neurobiology, have undermined the idea that gender differences are essential and biological, in order to challenge neurosexism, but they have not necessarily undermined the construct of gender itself. This means that on one hand Professor Fine has debunked the idea that women are "naturally" more caring, for example, but she has not yet necessarily challenged the whole idea of gender as a binary altogether. In fact, her work has been used both in support of and against the legitimacy of transgender and nonbinary identities. Other feminist scientists, like Sari van Anders, have moved in a different direction and are creating theories that strive to decenter cisgenderism altogether.

One such theory is indeed the Sexual Configurations Theory (SCT) by Dr van Anders. In this theory Sari van Anders creates a framework that centers lived experiences rather than theorized views of gender and sexuality. This means decentering cisgender and heterosexual identities as the baseline for what is considered the norm in relation to sexuality in particular. There is much more to this theory and you can check out the resources for Chapter 1 at the end of the book if you want to learn more about it. One of the revolutionary things about it is the decentering of cisgender male heterosexuality as the baseline within Western scientific discourse. What is important about this theory is that, rather than using evidence built on the same assumptions in relation to gender and sexuality, Dr van Anders is using it to change the foundations of how we conceptualize gender and sexuality themselves.

There is so much more to say about neuroscience and gender, but it would be beyond the scope of this book. For now let's just say that whatever the findings, one of the things that is important to consider when evaluating new evidence is what are the assumptions beneath it. In Chapter 2, I return to findings from neuroscience and how they are being used in public debate in ways that are particularly impactful for trans, nonbinary and gender expansive people.

It is important to notice that at the same time as scientists are tackling the construct of gender from neurobiological perspectives, other disciplines are also engaging with these ideas but from different perspectives. For example, there is a growing body of knowledge addressing gender from a decolonization perspective. It is to this that I turn next, returning to Indigenous perspectives, which is where we started this chapter from, because if gender, as we currently understand it, is indeed part of the ongoing settler colonial project, maybe we cannot dismantle gender essentialism within a colonial science paradigm.

 Educational stretch: finding our core assumptions

This seems to be a good moment to introduce our first "educational stretch." Whether you are a teacher, clinical supervisor, mentor or learner, take a moment to identify something you know for certain to be true about gender. This could be about the general construct of gender, your own gender, gender development in children, how gender plays out in couple dynamics or something you have observed in your peers when it comes to gender. What is it that you are sure of when it comes to gender? You just need one thing for this stretching exercise.

Once you have it, ask yourself the questions: "How do I know this to be true?" and "Why do I know this to be true?" Once you have answers, ask yourself these questions for each answer you have. Repeat this process until you arrive at what you consider to be core assumptions underlying the initial thing you knew to be true about gender. Are these assumptions you were aware of or not? Are they surprising or completely congruent with what you expected? If you want to stretch a little further, and especially if these assumptions surprise you, take a few more moments to reflect on where these assumptions come from. You might also want to consider what other beliefs might be built on these assumptions.

1.4 Decolonizing gender

In the previous section I argued that much of current Western science on gender is built either on the foundations of gender essentialism, and hence biological determinism, or on challenging these same foundations. These foundations, as argued throughout this chapter, are inextricably linked to a history of settler colonialism, in which colonizers use, more or less intentionally, theoretical frameworks focused on othering and separating to justify ownership and domination. If the roots of our oppression are multiple yet not separate as Audre Lorde has pointed out in much of her work, and if the "master's tools can never dismantle the master's house," as she stated in one of her most famous quotes (Lorde 1984/2007, p.112), then we need to change the frame when we look at gender as an aspect of

historical trauma, in order to collectively move towards account-
ability, repair and healing. I am indeed suggesting that a rigid
gender binary is one of the "master's tools," that is the colonizers'
tool, which has been systemically used to contribute not only to
gendered oppression but also to settler colonial and racialized
oppression.

Can authentic gender liberation then become part of the
decolonization many Indigenous scholars and activists have
called for? First let's take a moment to define decolonizing. At its
heart decolonization is about breaking free from the oppression
of settler colonialism physically and legally. This could mean
the removal of settlers. In places like Turtle Island, that is North
America, this can be complex as some settlers have been here for
numerous generations and no longer have a home anywhere else.
Decolonization here is seen by some, but not all, as decentering
European practices, knowledge, power and dominance.

I want to be clear though that for many Indigenous activists
and scholars decolonization is not considered possible or at least
complete until the land is returned into the custody of Indigenous people so decolonization "is not a metaphor" as Tuck and
Wayne-Yang (2012) remind us. Therefore even though I ultimately
believe that gender liberation needs to be part of a decolonizing
process, given that decolonizing has been co-opted as a metaphor by many non-Indigenous scholars, I also know that all I
can currently hope for is to invite us into a process of critical
awareness throughout this book. I do believe, and hope, that this
process can be part of a larger process of neurodecolonization
(Wilson and Bird 2012); that is, a process that as Pegi Eyers states:

> gently challenges the memes of Empire (western thinking) in
> our individual or collective consciousness, and replaces that

ideology or action with pre-colonial, or indigenous thinking. For ourselves, our families and our communities, the move toward life-enhancing and creative patterns, and compassionate and inclusive solutions, can be a life-long process. (Eyers 2017)

Therefore, recognizing that "we have all been colonized" as Eyers states in the same article—even though at different time—and that some of us are facing ongoing genocide, while others are not, how can we participate in decolonizing gender?

I have no answers, and binaohan (2014) has already offered a great critique of white gender theories and written a text for Indigenous and people of colour seeking to understand how their gender has been impacted by colonialism and whiteness. For a moment, though, I invite you to consider all trans, nonbinary and gender expansive people as well as every act of resistance to normative gender as wild weeds of restoration. Can part of a restoration process be as simple as recognizing the full humanity of all gender identities, expressions, roles and experiences? It seems simple, yet for this to be true on a systemic level, a dismantling of current legal, educational, social and cultural structures around gender would need to occur. This book is, in many ways, an invitation to do this. When I first came out as trans, I was often asked to educate other people about trans identities. As I have stated in other writing, I soon realized that everyone had a gender story to tell and that many of us were in pain because of dominant culture's rigidity when it comes to gender. I had already been learning from many Black (mostly women) authors I admired that our liberation is truly bound to one another. As Lilla Watson, a Gangulu visual artist, activist and scholar, reminds us in this often-used quote in activist communities: "But if you have come because your liberation is bound up with mine, then let us work together," although she feels this phrase was born from a collective process and credits it to the Aboriginal activists group, Queensland, 1970s.

Some Indigenous activists, in a similar vein, have been calling for non-Indigenous people to become accomplices and not allies. An accomplice has skin in the game and is prepared to be directly implicated. As stated in a zine/provocation by Indigenous Action (2014), "the work of an accomplice in anti-colonial struggle is to attack colonial structures and ideas." If a rigid gender binary is a colonial ideology, reproduced through colonial legal, political, economic and educational structures, how can we be accomplices in dismantling this in favor of an expansive paradigm in which we can all be in better relationship with our own and each other's genders? This is my explicit agenda in this book and in life. I believe that as mental health practitioners, providers and educators we can have a pivotal role in dismantling a hurtful, colonial, rigid gender binary, and can be accountable to one another, our communities and our clients as we engage in this ambitious process. In order to do so though we need to reckon with the ongoing legacy of the old paradigm. In the next chapter I examine more closely how the rigidity of the gender binary manifests as an aspect of historical trauma throughout our communities in a myriad of ways.

Summary

Here are the main points addressed in this chapter. Please note that many of these will be addressed again in more depth in the following chapters.

- Gender is a large biopsychosocial construct, which includes aspects of identity, expression, role and experience.
- Settler colonialism is an ongoing colonial project, in which the settlers' goal is to create structures that over time allow them to replace the Indigenous populations previously inhabiting the same space.
- Our current understanding of gender is deeply impacted by settler colonial practices, since gender itself seemed to historically be, in many Indigenous cultures, a concept more connected with identity, expression and role rather than biology.
- Controlling bodies, gender, relationships, language, culture and spirituality is an essential element of settler colonial states.
- A rigid gender binary is an aspect of historical trauma and the impact of the historical erasure of gender expansive people is experienced by people of all genders although the ways in which we are impacted are not the same.
- Gender essentialism is the ideology that tells us that men and women have certain characteristics that are inherent to their sex assigned at birth.
- The idea of gender essentialism itself rests on the larger concept of biological determinism. Biological determinism is the belief that our behaviors are connected to specific biological traits, such as genetics, physiology and so on.
- Much of current Western science on gender is built either on the foundations of gender essentialism, and hence biological determinism, or on challenging these same foundations.

- Decolonizing cannot be just treated as a metaphor. It is a process of systemic undoing and gender liberation can be viewed as part of a neurodecolonization process.
- In order to participate in decolonizing gender, those of us who are not Indigenous need to be prepared to be accomplices in dismantling a rigid gender binary as a form of colonial ideology.

CHAPTER 2

What's happening now?

In the previous chapter I considered how the ongoing settler colonial project has shaped ideas of gender and nurtured a rigid gender binary in multiple ways. In this chapter, my goal is to clearly lay out the ongoing impact that this has had, at least in Anglo dominant cultures. First of all you are invited to consider your own positionality, given that the impact does vary across communities. I then proceed to discuss gendered trauma as an aspect of the historical trauma impacting Indigenous communities on Turtle Island, currently widely known as North America. After this, I address how trans and/or nonbinary people are impacted in specific ways by rigid gender binaries and then flow into paying closer attention to the intersections of race, gender and ethnicity. I also attempt to weave other issues such as class and disability throughout the chapter. At the end of the chapter, I invite you to consider who, if anyone, benefits from a rigid gender binary system.

2.1 Positionality: locating ourselves

As I am writing this I live on Dakota and Anishinaabe land, currently known as Minnesota, Minneapolis, US. I was not always situated here. I grew up in Italy, mostly in Rome, but also spent significant amounts of time in Sicily, where my mother comes from. I spent my early adult years in England and then landed where I am now when I was in my late 30s. You may be asking yourself what this has to do with gender or this chapter. I am discussing my geographical location, both current and historical, because our understanding of gender is located in time and space. For example, there were definitely gendered expectations around me growing up but these were very different from the ones I experienced in my early 20s as an immigrant in the UK.

One of the gendered expectations growing up was that I would get married and have a child within a heterosexual relationship. However, this expectation from my maternal side of the family was at odds with familial reality, since several people assigned female at birth had never married in my family and education was highly prized by several family members. It was also at odds with cultural reality given that, due to economic decline, fewer and fewer young people were marrying and having children in Italy in the 1980s.

A different expectation emerged when I moved to England: I was often expected to have low-earning jobs and be less educated due to my ethnicity, class, immigrant status and gender. Even after disclosing that I was about to complete a PhD I was asked if I would be interested in a job as a bilingual nanny, for example. While my colleagues with Anglo-sounding names often secured stable academic jobs, I was not even invited to interview and went from contract position to contract position. Like many other feminine appearing and—at the time—identifying people, I also experienced gendered microaggressions, such as people not using my title, but using Dr in front of the name of male colleagues. Knowing how precarious my position in academia was, I was also more reluctant to take care of myself or work fewer hours, even as my health was declining while I headed towards what became a diagnosis of fibromyalgia.

The latter diagnosis presented new challenges. As a disabled person with an invisible chronic health condition, who was initially femme presenting, I was treated as a hypochondriac by several health providers. This was most definitely linked to my gender at the time, in fact so much so that a rheumatologist told me that once I "stopped working and had a baby" I would be less busy and stressed out, and apparently magically cured from fibromyalgia. I am pretty sure if I had been a cis man, I would never had been told to "go make a baby" as a way to manage my chronic health issues. Another provider told me it was "all in my head," which sounded very similar to accusations of hysteria that are still far too familiar to many women and femmes. After socially transitioning to a "masculine" presenting identity I faced other challenges, such as having expectations of physical strength I did not have placed on me. I have also been viewed as less "masculine" and continued to face ongoing misogyny partially due to my queer masculinity and nonbinary identity, but partially also due to the fact that, in dominant culture, disability is often viewed as "emasculating." Much as I do not subscribe to a binary idea of gender, I have had the experience of being treated in a range of ways because of the way my gender, and other aspects of my identity and experiences, have been read by those around me.

I am sharing these experiences to illustrate that our

positionality matters. Our geographical, historical, social, economic, somatic, racial and ethnic location intersects with gender in a myriad of ways, some visible and some less so. Both Black and disabled feminist scholars and activists had been drawing attention to this for a long time. In 1989, Black legal feminist scholar Kimberlé Williams Crenshaw coined the term intersectionality: a theoretical framework used to describe how different intersecting identities are systemically impacted in specific ways. Her initial work on this focused particularly on Black women in prison and how their experiences within both the legal and penal systems differed from those of both white women and Black men. However, this theoretical framework goes back much further. It is rooted in Black US history, such as Sojourner Truth's speech "Ain't I a Woman" given in 1851 at the Ohio Women's Rights Convention in Akron, which pointed out that the very way in which womanhood was being constructed and talked about excluded black women's lives.

The intersectionality framework has been expanded, is widely used and I have used it extensively in the past both in writing and in training. There are, however, other models to look at the intersections of power, privilege and oppression, such as Social Dominance Theory, which focuses on how group-based social dynamics and hierarchies are established, maintained and stabilized, or Hutchinson's analysis of intersectionality and its introduction of the construct of multidimensionality (2000). All these frameworks have their own validity and their relevance and appropriate use depends on our own positionality and the issues we are addressing.

Positionality is a concept that emerges from postmodern feminist theory and highlights the importance of explicitly stating our location given that there cannot be—within this framework—a disembodied, objective reader or writer. The construct of positionality is based on the assumption that all knowledge needs to be located; that is, we need to be able to identify where it came from, who produced it, why and in what contexts. Positionality also addresses aspects of identities, such as Indigeneity, race, gender, class and disability not as essential, intrinsic, static qualities but rather as relational and dynamic positions, which emerge and are maintained through relationships on micro (interpersonal) and macro (systemic) levels. Positionality is inextricably linked with reflexivity, given that the latter is essential for us to be able to articulate the former. Throughout this book, I draw on a range of the frameworks introduced here to address how gender intersects with other aspects of our lived experiences and identities, and how power, privilege and oppression are at play in various ways. Positionality is likely to be one of the main constructs I draw from and definitely the one I invite you to start from in this chapter.

When we view gender not just as a biopsychosocial construct but also as a position in time, space and community—that is, in a dynamic relationship to all other aspects of our lives and all aspects of our social structures—what does this open up and what does it close down? Let's take a moment to reflect on this further.

Thoughtful moment: mapping your relationship to gender

In the last chapter, you were invited to reflect on what you learned about gender from a historical perspective, as well as on what your core assumptions about gender are. Take a moment now to position both your own gender and your relationship to gender. If this sounds confusing, don't worry, I am about to break it down and guide you through this process.

First of all take a moment to list either out loud, in your mind or in writing how your own gender is positioned. For example, I was assigned female at birth by legal, cultural and social systems. I now identify as trans masculine and nonbinary: constructs that exist within specific linguistic, cultural and social systems. This is not how I am currently positioned legally, due both to personal beliefs as well as to constraints of the immigration system I am currently located within. All of these positions are inextricably connected to my ethnicity as an Italian person, as well as to my queerness, and class status that have led me to be both an economic and social migrant. I am also positioned as a mother in familial, cultural, social and legal contexts. I could probably add more dimensions to this map, such as how my disabilities and gender are positioned, but it's time for you to have some space to reflect on your own positionality with regards to gender. You might start by listing identity words, or you may want to consider larger systems, such as legal, educational, cultural, social, linguistic and so on. How is your gender located within yourself and within these systems? Which other aspects of your life come into play when you consider your gendered position?

Now let's consider your relationship to gender itself. For example, I have a relationship of curiosity with gender, as well as an academic relationship with gender. I also feel I have a clinical relationship to gender as a therapist and an educational relationship as an author, supervisor and trainer. What are the ways in which you relate to the construct of gender? Is this a construct that feels relevant to you or not? For example, you may identify as cisgender; that is, as someone whose gender assigned at birth aligns with their gender identity. Or you might identify as autigender; that is, you might see your understanding of gender as being connected to your neurodivergence. What is your relationship to gender? How has it changed over time, if at all? Is this a static or dynamic relationship? Have there been crucial moments in your relationship with gender? I hope that considering these questions can support you in identifying your own positionality as you read this book. You may of course be very clear on your positionality and, if this is the case, I still hope you have found some value in this thoughtful moment.

Now that I have spent some time providing a range of theoretical frameworks and we have considered both our own positionality and our relationship to gender as a construct, let's consider how people's positionality plays a role in how we are impacted by a rigid and essentialist gender binary. In the rest of the chapter this will be our focus.

First, given that an essentialist and rigid gender binary is part of the ongoing settler colonial project, I take some time to highlight how the current state of gender affairs is impacting Indigenous communities in the region we currently refer to as North America.

2.2 Impact of gendered trauma on Indigenous communities

In the previous chapter, I introduced the concept of historical trauma, a term used to indicate the cumulative impact of historical events that affect people from one generation to the next. This term was first coined and used, as stated earlier, in the 1980s by Lakota scholar Maria Yellow Horse Brave Heart. Since then, epigenetic scholars—that is, people looking at modification of gene expression and how this may alter organisms—have paid attention to historical trauma, sometimes also referred to as intergenerational or transgenerational trauma. The main point for the purposes of our discussion is that trauma can indeed be passed on from generation to generation. I purposefully use the term historical trauma rather than the alternative terms because some familial traumas, such as domestic violence, might be intergenerational and transgenerational, but they are not part of larger, specific historical events like the Holocaust or the Wounded Knee Massacre. That's what we're talking about here. Given that historical trauma is a term introduced by Indigenous scholars and that a rigid gender binary is part and parcel of the ongoing settler colonial process, it seems respectful to turn my attention to the impact of gendered trauma on Indigenous communities first.

One of the obvious and devastating impacts of historical trauma is the loss of language and culture. Enforced Christianization, combined with the systematic and ongoing separation of Indigenous children from their families—for example through residential schooling—have led to loss of language, including terms for a broader range of gender identities, roles and expressions, and loss of cultural, social and spiritual roles for gender expansive people within their own communities. The term Two-Spirit, which some of you might be familiar with, is an Anglo-based term that was coined in 1990 by people from many tribal nations at the Indigenous Lesbian and Gay International Gathering in Winnipeg. This was a term chosen with the intention of being for Indigenous people a culturally distinct term from existing terms. The need for this term to exist is in itself the legacy of the historical trauma of settler colonialism. Also, as stated before, not all Indigenous people use or identify with this term.

Part of the trauma is sadly visible in the violence, both individual and systemic, that Indigenous LGBTQ2 (lesbian, gay, bisexual, trans, queer, two-spirit) people experience. Despite the fact that data categorization often means that it is challenging to indicate exact numbers when discussing health disparities, these disparities clearly exist as can be seen both in existing reports and through the stories shared by Indigenous LGBTQ2 people themselves. As in many other minority groups, suicide rates, suicidal ideation, substance use, depression and anxiety tend to heavily impact Indigenous LGBTQ2 people as well as Indigenous communities generally. Indigenous LGBTQ2 people are sometimes further impacted if their tribal communities reject and/or isolate them on the basis of Christian values and gender essentialist ideals. They are also impacted by rejection, isolation and racism experienced within LGBTQ+ communities. Racism within LGBTQ+ communities can also manifest as exoticization and fetishization of Indigenous LGBTQ2 people, as well as of Black and Brown people generally. HIV rates might also be higher for Indigenous LGBTQ2 people, even though, once again, it is challenging to identify exact rates due to how data is collected. In Canada the rate of infection for Indigenous people is generally 3.5 times higher than for the non-Indigenous population. The higher rates of risk and infection are often coupled with lack of services for testing, prevention and care for HIV positive people. Younger Indigenous LGBTQ2 people are also likely to experience bullying, harassment and homelessness, as are all trans, queer and nonbinary youth. However, for Indigenous LGBTQ2 youth this is compounded by racism and impacted by the systemic and ongoing colonial violence experienced by their broader tribal communities.

Exploitation of Indigenous young people is experienced by both Indigenous LGBTQ2 people and by Indigenous girls. Where I currently live, for example, the report *Shattered Hearts*, published in 2009 (Pierce 2009), focused on the high rates of commercial sexual exploitation of Native women and girls in Minnesota. The report clearly indicates the root of this issue as lying in colonial understandings of Indigenous communities and the two racist and dangerous tropes that emerged at the beginning of the settler colonial project of Indigenous men as "ineffective and lazy" and of women as "sexually loose, mercenary, and innately immoral." The legacy of these tropes is still evident in the exploitation experienced especially by Indigenous girls who are often viewed as targets for commercial sexual exploitation. Indigenous girls, women and Two-Spirit people might also be more likely to engage in exchange sex, or sex work, for survival due to systemic poverty rather than by choice. This seems clear by some of the data presented in the report. For example, in Hennepin county, even though Indigenous women are only 2.2 percent of the general population, a quarter of sex work-related arrests in 2007 were of Indigenous women. Similar data can also be found in Canada. One of the factors that, for me, most clearly indicates that this is not just about higher rates of sex work amongst Indigenous women, is that the age of entry for a sizeable proportion of girls is around 8 to 12 years old. The Shattered Hearts report also clearly highlights how this is part of the legacy of generational/historical trauma, listing this, in fact, as the number one factor in the section on "factors that facilitate entry."

Exploitation though is only one part of the story. Another part that has become increasingly prominent in the media, albeit not yet sufficiently so, is the high rate of murdered and missing Indigenous women. In 2018, Lucchesi and Echo-Hawk wrote the report *Missing and Murdered Indigenous Women & Girls: A snapshot of data from 71 urban cities in the United States* as part of the *Our Bodies, Our Stories* series by the Urban Indian Health Institute, a tribal epidemiology center. They indicate how this is both a nationwide crisis and a data crisis given that, in 2016, out of 5712 cases of missing and murdered Indigenous women, only 116 were reported in Department of Justice federal database. The report states that murder is the third leading cause of death for Indigenous and Alaskan native women and girls. Many of these cases involved domestic and sexual violence, police brutality, and/or lack of safety for sex workers. Two percent of the cases involved homelessness as well as police brutality or death in custody. Just under 2 percent of the cases were trans women. Out of the perpetrators identified, 83 percent were male and about half were not Indigenous. Around a third of the perpetrators were not found guilty or were never considered accountable for their actions. The median age of the murdered and missing Indigenous women and girls is 29 years old, according to the report.

The report also highlighted how many law enforcement departments did not release data when requested to. Only one quarter of the cases of murdered and missing Indigenous women were covered by some form of local and/or national media and less than one fifth of the cases were covered more than once. The media coverage also often portrayed victims in a negative light by mentioning drugs or alcohol use, the victim's criminal history if she had one, and sex work, if this was involved. They gave false information, misgendered the victim when trans and even made excuses for the perpetrators or used victim-blaming language.

Indigenous LGBTQ2 people, women and girls on Turtle Island

are not the only Indigenous people facing gendered health dis-parities on a global level. Research in Australia focused directly on gendered health disparities amongst Aboriginal people and once again tied many of the disparities to the ongoing impact of colonization. This research also highlights how different the concept of gender is for Aboriginal people compared to Western patriarchal ideas of gender as a rigid and hierarchical binary. The displacement and dislocation from country—that is land—is viewed as a foundational contributing factor to the health disparities currently experienced by Aboriginal com-munities in Australia, given that gender in Aboriginal culture is deeply connected to relationship to country. For example, chronic disease, such as heart disease, type 2 diabetes or liver issues, contribute to a broad 75 percent gap in mortality rates between Indigenous and non-Indigenous men aged 35 to 54 in Australia. For men aged 55 to 74, the mortality gap rises to 95 percent. Once more, higher rates of substance use, alcoholism and tobacco use, which are generally higher among minority populations, also contribute to these disparities for Indigenous men. Although similar data does not seem readily available for Canada and the US, it is safe to assume that Indigenous men in North America are also experiencing health disparities given the systemic poverty, impact of police brutality and violence, and higher rates of substance use, tobacco use, alcohol use and mental health issues.

These numbers are heartbreaking, and might be even more so depending on your own positionality, so I invite you to take a moment to breathe. As I was writing this I asked myself whether it was necessary to list all this or if I was just another light-skinned person parading injured and dead Indigenous, Black and Brown bodies as props to make a point. I hope not, but I am also keenly aware of the impact this might be having on any Indigenous readers and I want to take a moment to acknowledge how different that impact is for non-Indigenous bodies. I also realize that my intention, which was to make sure those stories are visible to non-Indigenous readers, could be very far from my impact.

Breathe. Notice. Take it in. Whether this was new or familiar information, or anything in between. If you need to take care of yourself, please do so. This book will still be here when you are ready to continue. I truly invite you not to rush, gloss over or numb whatever feelings might be coming up, if you are not an Indigenous person. This is the landscape in which many of us live, work, educate, counsel, heal. I believe non-Indigenous providers need to be able to honestly look at it if we are to be effective in our roles. So, really, I mean it; take the time you need before we proceed as more heart-breaking facts are laid out in the rest of this chapter, hopefully not for us to gawk at but to realize the scope of the gendered trauma we are immersed in across a range of communities.

2.3 Trans and/or nonbinary people and gendered trauma

Before I started writing this book, I would talk about it and often people assumed that this was a book around trans people and our trauma. I can understand that assumption, given my identity. Later in this section I go through some facts that make it pretty clear that trans and/or nonbinary people, and especially BIPOC (Black, Indigenous People of Color) trans and/or nonbinary people, are heavily impacted by cisgenderism and gender essentialism. To begin with, let's take a moment to consider how trans and/or nonbinary people are impacted by rigid gender binaries in a range of ways.

I am using the umbrella terms trans and/or nonbinary because not everyone who identifies as nonbinary also identifies as trans, although some of us do, and because there are trans people who identify with a binary construct of gender. One of the painful ways in which rigid constructs of the gender binary are showing up in our communities is the internal divisions. A decade or more ago, although this still happens, it used to be that some people would distinguish between "true transsexual" people and other trans people who were not as dedicated to passing or accessing body modification through surgery. More recently, and vastly in reaction to the historical erasure and belittling of trans, agender and/or nonbinary people, the term "truscum" emerged. This term is used to indicate those who think that dysphoria is an essential component of being trans and that anyone who identifies as trans but does not experience dysphoria is not really trans. This has also given rise to the term "trans trender," especially among younger people, to indicate people who "say they're trans because it's trendy or because they want attention." When I first came across this term what was very evident to me was the fact that these were words I had heard cis parents, therapists and educators use over and over again about trans and/or nonbinary youth. These were the arguments often offered by cis adults to invalidate young trans and/or nonbinary people's experiences and identities. They are also similar to the "true transsexual" narrative, which seemed to be well aligned with views from the medical-industrial complex, where experts were ready to tell us who was "truly" trans and who was not. Why is it important to notice this when talking about gendered trauma in trans and/or nonbinary communities?

In many ways these internal divisions, often encouraged and exploited by people who do not have the wellbeing of trans and/ or nonbinary communities at heart, are a symptom of collective trauma. From the early 1900s in Berlin when Magnus Hirschfeld first coined the term transvestite and later developed the Berlin Institute where the first "sex change" operations took place, to the later creation of the term transsexual in the late 1940s, the gender identities, expressions and roles of trans and/or non-binary people have been heavily defined and policed by white cisgender experts. Up to 20 years ago in what we currently call the US, trans people had to go up for examination by a panel to assess whether they were ready for hormones and/or surgical intervention, if they wished to pursue medical transition. Currently in many countries, such as the UK, trans and/or nonbinary people are still dependent on a specialist declaring that they are feminine or masculine enough—characteristics usually defined within a colonial, white supremacist framework—to access any medical interventions. In the UK and several other countries if trans people are married, their spouse needs to agree to any medical interventions. In some countries, such as Sweden until 2012, trans people had to undergo sterilization before they were "allowed" to access any medical interventions. Given that as trans and/or nonbinary people we were told that our condition was a mental health issue and that only specialists could decide whether we were well enough, despite our diagnosis, to access any medical and/or legal services, it is no surprise that our communities have internalized some of these ideas and then turned on to one another.

This seems a clear case of trauma generating trauma. If your gender is scrutinized, policed, streamlined by cis white people who have clear binary expectations of gender and who are literally telling you what is a legitimate way to walk, dress, talk, do your hair or make up, and who are telling you that if you disagree with their advice, it clearly demonstrates you're mentally unwell, hostile and sick, it seems reasonable that you might end up internalizing some of these ideas. I often talk about systemic oppression being like the air we breathe. We do not even notice it is getting into our lungs and becoming part of us, yet there it is. Sadly this means that some of us have adopted management strategies that include policing other people, just like we have been historically policed. The borders of gender might change as might the methods but the issue of containing gender expansiveness remain.

As a somatic practitioner I know that trauma often means we contract, make ourselves smaller, freeze or even disappear for survival. Our collective soma is contracted around gender. It's as if we're all holding a collective breath and breathing as shallowly as we can because we're afraid of what might happen if we let go and breathe freely. Unfortunately when we have, unpleasant things have historically happened and are still happening.

Going back to Berlin in the early 1900s, for example, the work of Hirschfeld was emerging within a community where people, at least middle- and upper-class white people, had the freedom to express their gender and sexuality in more expansive ways. Soon after this, the rise of the Third Reich began. It was preceded by a period of tightening of moral values, a contracting of possibilities, and eventually a rounding up of trans, nonbinary, queer and gender expansive people of all ethnicities. While not forgetting that the Holocaust mostly and massively impacted Jewish people all over Europe, I also want to acknowledge that many disabled, trans, nonbinary, queer, and gender expansive people were also targeted during this time.

In more recent history, it suffices to look at all the names we remember each Transgender Day of Remembrance in November to realize that our community is not yet safe, especially for our BIPOC siblings. Most of the names we read are of trans feminine people of color, and those are just the names we know. It also does not include those of us who died by suicide: an epidemic that impacts us in rates ten times higher than the general population, probably due to the systemic erasure and oppression experienced by our communities.

The rates of harassment, violence and murder are indeed high for trans and/or nonbinary communities. In the US-based report *Injustice at Every Turn*, published by the National Center for Transgender Equality and the National Gay and Lesbian Task Force in 2011, which is one of the largest surveys to date with 6450 participants, the authors found that all respondents experienced discrimination but the combination of transphobia and racism was particularly harmful.

Other findings indicated that trans and/or nonbinary people tend to live in poverty or be, at least, underemployed; we might lose jobs more easily (over half the participants had lost jobs); be harassed or bullied in school (with 51% of participants reporting this); or experience physical or sexual assault (61% and 64% of participants had experienced this). We are also less likely to seek healthcare given that we experience higher rates of discrimination by healthcare providers, including being refused care due to our gender identities and/or expression. Understandably many of the participants managed this by either hiding their gender identity or transition history (71% of respondents) and/ or by postponing any transition processes (57% of respondents).

If our gender identities and expressions put us in danger then "passing" in any direction—that is by transitioning and hiding within the other end of the spectrum, or by delaying transitioning and being assumed to be cisgender—can become a means of survival in a world that can feel impossible to exist in. Once more, this is even more so for our BIPOC siblings, whose safety is far more in danger when deviating from societal gender norms. As trans and nonbinary people we're effectively caught in a double bind given that performing within the range of the binary leads to societal validation and legitimation. However, holding a construct of gender that is too rigid ultimately leads to higher levels of internalized transphobia, lower self-esteem and potentially related mental health issues in our communities.

It is also not surprising to see in the report higher rates of participation in sex work and other kinds of underground economy among trans people, given the frequent lack of job security as well as the higher rates of poverty in our communities. Once again, the intersection of gender with class, race, ethnicity, Indigeneity, disability and citizenship status amplifies any of the experiences and percentages listed so far. Trans and/or nonbinary people also experience higher rates of HIV risk and infection, while not always having access to relevant and competent services for prevention, testing and care for positive people. Research also shows higher rates of depression, anxiety, tobacco use and substance use. The survey initially reported was expanded and repeated a few years later and 27,715 people participated this time. This time the survey was also available in both English and Spanish. Sadly the findings remained frighteningly close to the previous one.

You are likely to find similar issues for minority populations again and again. From a trauma perspective this makes sense. When our collective and individual soma contracts we're more prone to go into either collapse or sympathetic nervous system activation, which aligns with labels such as depression or anxiety. Often they might both occur at once, making us feel like we're simultaneously pushing down on the brakes while feeling completely revved up inside. Research has also shown us that addiction is a disease of intimacy, so it makes sense that if we're told or shown that we do not belong or that we're not safe, many people self-medicate through tobacco use and/ or substances such as alcohol, recreational drugs or abuse of prescription drugs. If we're intolerable to society, how can we learn to accept ourselves fully? If we're seen as a disease, how can we not feel a lack of ease in our own selves? If one in ten of us, for trans and/or nonbinary people, had a family member be violent towards us after coming out and many even lost our homes, how can we feel at home with ourselves?

Clinical vignette: dealing with internalized transphobia

Initially I was reluctant to place a clinical vignette in the section addressing the impact of rigid gender binaries on trans and/or nonbinary people. After all, one of the issues that we face is that of pathologization! However, I decided that I really wanted to discuss addressing internalized transphobia in the therapy room from a trans perspective. Far too often I have come across cisgender therapists who seem to think that the answer to internalized transphobia is just to love ourselves. While I believe that self-love is indeed to be nurtured for everyone, I also wanted to approach this issue from a more critical stance. So, without further ado, here's a clinical vignette with some questions and ideas for reflection and practice. I hope you'll find this helpful.

"Eider is a nonbinary person in their early 30s. They're out to family, friends and co-workers and feel supported by most of them. Eider doesn't really think that many of their people truly understand their nonbinary identity, but all their close people respect Eider's pronouns (they/them). They have been really struggling with decisions around body modification, such as cross-sex hormones and surgical interventions. Eider is not sure if they truly want them or if they just want them to better fit in a world that is still very binary. They're scared of looking and feeling 'like a freak' no matter what. Eider is also struggling not just with dysphoria but with a history of disordered eating and body image issues. They're feeling stuck and frustrated."

One of the first interventions that might come to mind is to really focus on Eider's body image issues. For example, you might suggest to Eider to notice what kind of media they're consuming. What is their visual diet, and might this be contributing to Eider's lack of ease with their body? You might ask Eider to keep a gratitude journal focusing on what their body can do rather than what they look like. Another intervention might be to ask Eider to start noticing the negative self-talk and to challenge this with more rational and kinder thoughts. You might even ask Eider to write a letter from their future self to their current self to explain the decisions they have made, why they have made them and how these decisions have impacted them. These are all great and worthwhile interventions and I have used all of these with my clients at various points in time.

However, let's take a moment longer to reflect on whether, alongside these interventions, something else might be needed. All the interventions above are focused on developing further an internal locus of control—that is, the belief system about causes of our experiences. Generally psychological research shows that people with a well-developed internal locus of control are more confident in their ability to change and influence situations and might even have higher self-esteem. It would make sense then to focus on nurturing an internal locus of control when Eider is dealing with so many body image issues. This is one of these moments when I invite you to consider a both/and approach.

While it's true that addressing negative self-cognition is important, it's also important to explicitly acknowledge that Eider is not only dealing with shadows in their thoughts but with a world that is truly challenging for nonbinary people. Not acknowledging the latter is akin to gaslighting Eider. Their concerns are legitimate, as is their dance with where their desire for body modification comes from. Addressing this can be done in a range of ways. From a narrative therapy perspective, you could spend time mapping with Eider all the different macro influences on their sense of self and their desire for body modification. What is dominant culture telling them: the media, language, the faith community they might have been brought up in? What are the stories about Eider's identities out there that have an influence on their internal sense of self?

You can also support Eider in thinking through consequences of different actions. For example, what does each type of body modification open up and what does it close down for Eider? If the desire for some changes is more about ease in navigating a binary world, can that be ok? Often trans and/or nonbinary people can feel pressured to be the poster child of the movement and, as such, to be confident and self-accepting at all costs. This can be incredibly difficult in a world that is, in reality, rife with harassment and even violence for gender expansive, feminine presenting people of color like Eider. What difference can it make when we acknowledge this in therapy?

You may want to invite Eider to consider whether their decisions need to be perfect. Is there something other than an all-or-nothing approach available here? Can it be possible to have an ideal but to make a compromise with the reality we live in? What if sometimes the trans or nonbinary body is not quite what we would want ideally but rather a compromise or approximation of what we would ideally want? I know I felt a huge weight lift when a therapist talked to me about my body being a compromise in some ways. I notice a similar relief in several clients who might have a more ambivalent relationship with the idea of body modification. Basically, what becomes possible when we acknowledge that while there is indeed an internal locus of control, there is also a world out there that is not always friendly or even safe for many of our trans and/or nonbinary clients? What other interventions might you consider from a both/and approach to these issues? What is the positionality of your clients, and how does it impact them within both trans and/or nonbinary communities, and within larger, local community? What is your positionality and how does it impact your therapeutic choices in this case?

In addition to the systemic harassment, violence and oppression experienced, trans and/or nonbinary people have been increasingly subject to vehement attacks by people who are often referred to as TERFs: trans-exclusionary radical feminists. Much has already been written about the term, whether it can be considered a slur or not, and on whether it is even ever feminist to exclude trans people from the movement. It is beyond the scope of this book to enter into an in-depth debate about this issue. However, I do want to take a moment to look at this phenomenon from a trauma perspective.

As I stated at the beginning of this section, trauma can generate trauma, especially when unaddressed. I believe that many people who embrace TERF ideology, which conflates sex with gender and is ultimately a gender essentialist ideology, have been hurt by a rigid gender binary. Unfortunately rather than realizing the impact of settler colonial, patriarchal, misogynistic oppression, people who embrace TERF ideology view trans people as part of the problem and often even as "oppressors." Instead of viewing the rigid policing of bodies as the issue, they adopt a rigid conceptualization of gender based on biology and conflate genitals with identity and experience.

This seems to be a manifestation of the roots of white Anglo feminism in many ways. If the baseline for the feminist movement is a cis white, often but not exclusively straight, woman, then anyone who does not fall in these categories deviates from the norm. Just as the early white Anglo feminist movement did not include Black and Brown women—as indicated by the history of suffragettes and the writing of many Black feminists and the creation of womanism—and later struggled to include lesbian and bi women, it is still struggling to expand to include anyone who is impacted by patriarchal, cisgenderist and rigid binary views of gender. Some aspects of white feminism are so contracted, due to historical trauma, that expansion seems not only undesirable but dangerous. This can be viewed in the rhetoric used by many TERFs, which evokes images of rape, assault and general danger to instil a sense of fear towards trans and/or nonbinary people and our allies. As I have written in an article on "Gender and Sexual Legitimacy" in 2015 (p.105):

trans bodies then seem to become the battlefield on which the expansion of our conceptualization of gender seems to be played, as Stryker points out in her essay on Biopolitics where she discusses trans as a category to be monitored by the bio-power, which is actively invested in promoting and maintaining normativity in all bodies, including trans bodies.

Rhetoric of fear is often a tool used to contain, mainstream and keep people in line with the status quo. It is understandable that if we feel under threat, we might want to not rock the boat. We might prefer keeping things stable and protecting ourselves through both a freeze and contracted response in our soma. It is no accident that TERF ideology seems to be so closely aligned with what many BIPOC feminists have clearly labeled white feminism. Therefore, it is to the intersection of gender, race and ethnicity that I want to turn next.

2.4 The intersection of gender, race and ethnicity

In the previous section I mentioned white feminism. Depending on your positionality you may find yourself bristle at coupling a racial qualifier to the feminist movement, or you may feel that it is a familiar phrase that you understand. Let's revisit positionality for a moment. If positionality views identities as dynamic and relational, then it makes sense that our feminism is not independent from our positionality. In fact one of the assumptions to consider when talking about larger movements, such as feminism, is who is, by definition, included and who is not. Feminism as it emerges in Western dominant Anglo contexts and history is inextricably linked, in some ways, to whiteness. Womanhood might have been addressed as a univer-sal concept but even in the earliest days of women's rights and suffrage, the term was not universal in praxis. Womanhood too often meant white womanhood and I would add abled, middle- to upper-class womanhood. There is a reason why Sojourner Truth, mentioned earlier, was addressing the issue of both her womanhood and Blackness as far back as 1851 when addressing the Women's Convention in Akron, Ohio.

I would argue that gender is always dependent on intersec- tions of other aspects of our identities, such as class, disability, citizenship, Indigeneity, race and ethnicity. After all what is considered masculine or feminine is heavily dependent on spe- cific historical, geographical, economic and social locations. Of course, disabled, Indigenous, Black and Brown women have been addressing this issue for a long time. For example, Gloria Evange- lina Anzaldúa, a Chicana lesbian scholar, wrote about the spaces between genders and sexuality, as well as ethnicity and geog- raphy, in the foundational text published in 1987: *Borderlands/ La Frontera: The New Mestiza*. A few years earlier Black US-based writer and activist Alice Walker used the term womanist in a short story (Walker 2011). The term womanism was then adopted by many Black women as a theoretical framework specifically based on the experiences and history of Black women. Just two years after Alice Walker used the term womanist, in 1981, bell hooks published *Ain't I a Woman?: Black Women and Feminism*, titled after Truth's speech (hooks 1981/2014). It would, once again, be beyond the scope of this book to fully address the history of feminism and the critical approaches to feminism led by Black and Brown women, as well as trans women, and disabled wom- en such as Jenny Morris who published *Pride Against Prejudice: Transforming Attitudes to Disability* in 1991 and Julia Serano's *Whipping Girl: A Transsexual Woman on Sexism and the Scapegoating of Femininity* (2016), first published in 2007. These are all seminal texts which I invite you to read, if you have not done so already, in order to understand just how much women at the margins of dominant society have contributed to feminism, as this is not always visible. For now, let's focus in on how the intersection of race, ethnicity and gender impacts people every day.

Systemic poverty due to historical factors, such as slavery and ongoing racism, has contributed to health disparities around specific conditions such as asthma, diabetes and heart disease for Black people living in what we currently know as the US. Black people in the US also experience higher rates of cancer and stroke, with these and heart disease being leading causes of death. Black women in particular are often at higher risk of dying of heart disease because the symptoms are not recognized early enough. They are also more likely to die of diseases such as breast cancer, and to be diagnosed less often than in white women. Black women are also two to six times more likely to die of complications from childbirth. Education or income seem to make little difference in this regard, highlighting how dangerous the mix of racism and misogyny is. This means that educated, high-earning Black women are still more likely to die from complications from childbirth even when compared to less educated and poor white women. I highlight this in order to dismantle one of the false beliefs that all racial disparities stem purely from economic and class disparities. This is also evident when considering the issue of pain management and Black people. The latter tend to be undertreated for pain due to healthcare providers holding implicit bias and inaccurate racist beliefs about biological differences between Black and white people.

It is unsurprising that healthcare providers would hold such implicit bias and racist beliefs. After all scientists, biologists and physicians have historically perpetuated false and racist beliefs about inherent biological differences between Black and white people, such as, but not limited to, less sensitivity to pain. You might think that these beliefs would be behind us, but it is enough to critically read articles about Black athletes to notice the implicit racist beliefs about fundamentally different characteristics between Black and white bodies. This means that stereotypes such as the "strong Black woman" are not just metaphorically hurtful; they can literally mean that a Black woman is less likely to be taken seriously when in pain or to seek medical care in the first place given the level of harassment and discrimination experienced. Black men might also less likely to receive appropriate pain treatment due to stereotypes around drug use and being viewed as pill-seeking. The latter shows how different, racist stereotypes can also combine to negatively impact Black people's everyday life. If Black people in general are supposed to be stronger and masculinity is also about being strong, then Black men are not likely to be believed when reporting pain. At this point the false perceptions around race and gender intersect with stereotyping around drug use, resulting in Black men being less likely to be prescribed appropriate treatments such as opioids even when in severe pain.

Media coverage of Black women athletes also highlights how Black women are more likely to be viewed as aggressive and, as such, as less feminine. This can lead to close scrutiny of Black women athlete bodies, as has happened again and again during various Olympic competitions. In everyday life this can also lead to pressure to perform femininity in a certain way in order to be perceived as a "legitimate woman" or otherwise risk having one's gender questioned. This is particularly impactful of course for queer, trans and/or nonbinary Black women but it can impact any

Black woman, regardless of gender and sexuality. These harmful tropes of Black women as less feminine, stronger and hypersexual lead to real danger for Black women in everyday life, especially, but not exclusively, for butch women and trans women. This is the danger of confrontation and harassment on the street as well as in schools, at work or in sports, a confrontation and harassment that is often only a heartbeat away from more lethal violence. The latter seems to be particularly relevant when noticing the level of police brutality, including murder, experienced by Black people of all genders in what we currently call the US.

Other factors contributing to those already described are also geographical location and religion. For example, Islamophobia greatly contributes to violence towards Muslim people or people perceived to be Muslim. This is true not just in North America but, currently, seems to be the case globally. On one hand Muslim women are often depicted in Western media as a patriarchal archetype of female subjugation, taking away any agency they have over their own religious beliefs and gender presentation. On the other hand, Muslim women are often harassed or attacked if they wear visible signs of their religion, such as a hijab. Their ethnicity and religion combined contributes to them no longer being viewed as "feminine" and therefore "weak" and "not to be struck" according to social gendered scripts in Western dominant culture. In fact, race and ethnicity seem to be powerful lenses when applied to gender given that, in Western dominant culture, the baseline is viewed as Anglo, cisgender, heterosexual and abled. I have already highlighted how this has meant that Indigenous men are viewed as being emasculated by women because of the lack of gendered hierarchical patriarchal structure. However, there are numerous tropes and stereotypes that illustrate this point. For example, Asian women are often viewed in Western dominant culture as inherently more docile, passive and subservient than white women, another dangerous trope that can lead to harassment, violence and exploitation.

It seems safe to state that generally Black, Brown and Indigenous bodies are often hypersexualized, such as the stereotype of the "hot-blooded" Latina woman, while also being scrutinized for gender ambiguities and discrepancies. The examples could sadly go on and on but suffice to state that common experiences seem to be higher rates of harassment, discrimination and violence, poorer health outcomes, and health disparities. The flavor of the stereotypes and violence does differ according to specific positionality but they do seem to be variations on a theme that views the cisgender, white, abled, heterosexual body as the baseline and a rigid gender binary as the picket fence around it that needs to be defended at all costs.

Educational stretch: what are the gendered expectations in your communities?

I've provided information about how rigid gender binaries impact several minority communities. The communities you belong to may or may not have been represented in the information offered so far. If I have discussed communities you belong to, take a moment to reflect on the information offered. This might have been very familiar to you and you may even have more information than this chapter can offer. Take a moment to notice the information and how it impacts you and your work. Does this information shape the way you address clients, students, patients, co-workers or community members?

If I have not discussed any or some of the communities you

belong to, take a moment to consider how gendered expectations impact individuals within those communities and how they shape the community itself. You may want to do some research if you're not familiar with information about the impact of gender norms in your communities. Google Scholar can be a good place to start and you can use keywords such as gender, disparities, health, education and so on, depending on the areas you're interested in.

Finally, take a moment to reflect on what the physical, psychological, emotional and spiritual impact of rigid gender norms is on you and your communities. How does this shape you and your work in the world? What becomes possible if you step outside of these norms and what might be the cost of doing so?

2.5 Does anyone benefit?

At this point you might assume that at least white, cisgender, abled, heterosexual people would benefit from the settler colonial, rigid gender binary. However, that is not necessarily the case as (cis)gender normativity benefits surprisingly few people! Although deviating further away from the gender binary, as many visibly nonbinary, gender expansive and defiant people do, entails a higher risk of encountering harassment and violence, the borders of gender are diligently patrolled for everyone. For example, several studies have concluded that gender conformity—which often entails the need for approval and validation from others—can negatively affect psychological wellbeing, as well as hinder sexual autonomy.

This can be noticed in increasingly understood terms such as toxic masculinity, for example, as well as in gendered behaviors and scripts performed by feminine people to uphold said toxic masculinity within a patriarchal framework. Let's take a moment to break this down. If being a man in Anglo dominant white culture means being not emotionally expressive, for example, men are going to be less likely to seek support when facing mental health challenges. They are also more likely to become depressed, if they are previously abled, and then become disabled, since the latter is not compatible with the dominant construct of masculinity as "strong, tough, and independent." Even without any disabilities or mental health challenges present, we know from therapeutic literature that internalizing emotions, rather than expressing them authentically at least with people close to us, is not conducive to genuine relationships and can, in fact, contribute to feelings of isolation and decreased psychological wellbeing, as found in a number of studies. Even though we know from neurobiology that consensual and healthy touch is essential to our wellbeing as humans, men, within a more rigid binary patriarchal framework, can only give and receive touch through sex or sports. Research has also shown us that men are often less likely to seek and access healthcare, even when needed. For example, the World Health Organization reported that suicide represented half of all male violent deaths worldwide in 2017. Women suffer high rates of depression and disordered eating, among other issues, which I explore in the chapter on relationships.

I could cite more research on how rigid gender binaries negatively impact the psychological and physical wellbeing of cisgender white people. The main point is that even though some people are definitely much more impacted by the legacy of a rigid gender binary than others—and those most impacted are definitely Black, Brown, Indigenous, immigrant, disabled, trans and queer people, especially feminine ones—nobody wins in this arena. This is not new information. Sandra Bem dedicated much of her work to highlighting how gender roles and gender polarization contribute to inequalities and contribute to poor psychological wellbeing (see Bem 1993). However, even Bem's work was steeped in an earlier feminist rhetoric that viewed egalitarianism and equality as goals, rather than seeking the dismantling of a rigid gender binary as a settler colonial patriarchal tool that contributes to the control and policing of our collective soma.

Social control is challenging to undermine as it is not just perpetuated through larger structures, such as legislation, governance, education or healthcare, but it is most often passed on from one generation to the next. Another important part of Bem's legacy is that she pointed out how important it is to challenge rigid gender schema—that is, roles or ideas—in children, if we aspire to move towards a more egalitarian society. Even though the goal of gender liberation is, within this framework, about neurodecolonization rather than egalitarianism within the current, ongoing settler colonial paradigm, the issue of how we raise our children is still salient. Therefore I turn to intergenerational patterns in the next chapter.

Summary

Before moving on to the next chapter, here are the main points addressed in this chapter:

- Our understanding of gender is located in time and space. This means it is important to pay attention to our positionality.

- Positionality is a concept that emerges from postmodern feminist theory highlighting the importance of explicitly stating our location given that there cannot be a disembodied, objective reader or writer.
- One of the impacts of a rigid gender binary on Indigenous communities in North America has been the loss of language and culture, including terms for a broader range of gender identities, roles and expressions, and loss of cultural, social and spiritual roles for gender expansive people within their own communities.
- Indigenous LGBTQ2 people as well as broader Indigenous populations face higher rates of health disparities, mental health issues, tobacco and substance use, as well as higher risk of HIV infection.
- Younger Indigenous LGBTQ2 people are also likely to experience bullying, harassment and homelessness, as are all trans, queer and nonbinary youth.
- Indigenous women, girls and Indigenous LGBTQ2 people are more likely to be murdered, including dying in police custody and due to police brutality, or go missing. Those cases are under-reported and media often uses victim-blaming language.
- The displacement and dislocation from country, in other words land, is viewed as a foundational contributing factor to the health disparities currently experienced by Aboriginal communities in Australia, given that gender in Aboriginal culture is deeply connected to relationship to country.
- Internal divisions and othering within trans and/or nonbinary communities are rooted in intergenerational trauma and have been impacted by the long history of

pathologization experienced by trans and/or nonbinary people at the hands of the medical-industrial complex.

- Trans and/or nonbinary people are ten times more likely than the general population to struggle with suicidality and are at higher risk of dying by suicide.
- Trans and/or nonbinary people experience higher rates of discrimination, harassment, physical and sexual assault, bullying in school and refusal of care by healthcare providers.
- Trans and/or nonbinary people are at higher risk of HIV infection, are more likely to be HIV positive and are more likely to be involved in underground economies, such as sex work. They're also often living in poverty and/or underemployed.
- Since positionality views identities as dynamic and relational, it makes sense that our feminism is not independent from our positionality. Black, Brown, disabled and trans scholars have critically approached feminism and highlighted places where the movement has historically been exclusionary.
- Systemic poverty due to historical factors, such as slavery and ongoing racism, has contributed to health disparities around specific conditions such as asthma, diabetes and heart disease for Black people in the US. They also experience higher rates of cancer and stroke, with these and heart disease being leading causes of death.
- Black women are two to six times more likely to die of complications from childbirth, regardless of education or income.
- Black women's gender is more likely to be questioned

and closely scrutinized, which can lead to higher rates of harassment and violence.

· Black people, including women and especially trans women, are more likely to be murdered by the police, die in police custody or due to police brutality.

· Islamophobia greatly contributes to global violence towards Muslim people or people perceived to be Muslim. Muslim women are more likely to be harassed or attacked for wearing visible signs of their cultural and/or religious affiliation such as a hijab.

· Black, Brown and Indigenous bodies are often hypersexualized, while also being scrutinized for gender ambiguities and discrepancies.

· Several studies have concluded that gender conformity, which often entails the need for approval and validation from others, can negatively affect psychological wellbeing, as well as hinder sexual autonomy.

· Toxic masculinity leads to poorer health for cis men. For example, research has shown us that cis men are often less likely to seek and access healthcare, even when needed.

CHAPTER 3

All in the family

In the previous chapter I have attempted to portray how a rigid gender binary negatively impacts a number of people, especially Black, Brown, Indigenous, immigrant, disabled, trans and queer bodies, and intersections thereof. I also briefly mentioned that trauma can be intergenerational, sometimes also called transgenerational, and that this is sometimes connected to, but distinct from, historical trauma.

In this chapter, I start from definitions of intergenerational and transgenerational trauma and discuss epigenetics and why it might matter, as well as how its use, in the context of trauma, has been criticized. After this, I consider what kinds of gendered stories, patterns and roles might be passed on and how they're passed on. I also briefly discuss the role of shame and blame within intergenerational trauma, as well as the ways in which intergenerational gendered trauma can impact our attachment styles. Finally, I consider the role of ancestral connection and its role for individual and collective resilience.

3.1 What is epigenetics and why it matters (maybe)

The first chapter laid out how a rigid gender binary can be viewed as an aspect of historical trauma linked to patriarchal settler colonial understandings of gender. In the second chapter I addressed what the manifestations of this trauma are and mentioned briefly how historical trauma is not the same as intergenerational trauma. The latter is where I want to start from for this chapter. Although historical trauma is, by definition, intergenerational, given that it is passed on from generation to generation in a range of ways, including through lasting social, linguistic and cultural patterns, not all intergenerational trauma is historical, at least not in this definition of historical. For example, certain things might have happened in one family, such as domestic violence, and the impact might have been passed on from one generation to the next. While there is a social and historical context to this trauma, this is specific to this family and it does not involve a larger-scale historical event like the Rwandan genocide or slavery. The main distinction then is that historical trauma is collective, and it involves many people beyond an individual family line.

However, what happens in individual family lines does not happen outside of history or culture. This is one of the reasons why we're looking at the complexity of a rigid gender binary as trauma. Trauma is not only transmitted through larger historical and social patterns but also in the everyday interactions we experience from day one of our lives, and some would say even in utero. The field of epigenetics, in particular, has attempted to document how historical and intergenerational trauma is not just passed on from parent to child through behaviors and relationships, but also through our genes. Epigenetics is the study of how modifications of gene expressions cause changes, rather than the study of changes in the genetic code itself. Some scientists believe that not only do we receive our DNA from our biological parents but that we also inherit information on how genes might switch on or off, that is, express themselves. One of the most recent and popular studies in this area was conducted by Rachel Yehuda and team who studied both Holocaust survivors and children of Holocaust survivors (Shalev, Yehuda and McFarlane 2000). They found that genetic mutation can happen quickly and that the impact of trauma can be felt from one generation to the next. The study was highly publicized by the media, but it also drew heavy criticism in the field of epigenetics. Some scientists felt that the sample was too small, that it excluded social factors that could be important to consider, and that heritability mechanisms could not be clearly established as a consequence of this study.

Whether you consider the study to withstand scrutiny or not, several scholars and clinicians over the years have observed the phenomenon of generations being impacted by the trauma of the previous generation. Initially this was referred to as transgenerational as it focused on trauma being passed on from one generation to the next. However, once people started addressing effects in the third generation and beyond, the term intergenerational came into play. For the purposes of this chapter, I use the word intergenerational given that I will not just be looking at transmission from one generation to the next one. The Holocaust, the enslavement of African people for the benefit of the colonies, and the decimation of Indigenous populations in what is currently known as North America are probably amongst the most studied historical phenomena when it comes to intergenerational trauma. Scholars studying these phenomena noticed that, although families and individuals had a role to play—and how families reacted to events could make a difference—there were common experiences and symptoms people have when they shared a collective traumatic experience.

For example, Dr. Degruy-Leary (1994) identified a phenomenon they called Post-Traumatic Slave Syndrome (PTSS) to indicate the psychological and emotional trauma from slavery. PTSS clearly delineates how the past has an ongoing impact on the present for Black people in the US. Some scholars believe that this has been an under-estimated factor when it comes to considering social disparities, for example, and that there are clinical implications of PTSS for therapists and providers to consider. Others, like Hicks, highlight that Black people have also inherited resilience and healing, and not just trauma, and that instead of hyper-pathologizing Black people, future studies could focus on the mental health status of the oppressors as well as on the "legacies of survival, resilience, transcendence, and healing birthed out of the historical trauma of slavery" (Hicks 2015, p.v). The idea that we do not just inherit trauma intergenerationally but also resilience and strategies for our survival is one that I consider to be incredibly relevant and important, so I return to it at the end of this chapter to address it in more depth. PTSS is clearly a form of historical trauma. What about forms of intergenerational trauma that do not fall under the umbrella of historical trauma though?

Whether epigenetics has yet proven whether intergenerational trauma exists or not, to many practitioners it seems evident that there are patterns in how humans respond to trauma, which seem to emerge again and again in minority populations, as well as in individuals who have a history of intergenerational trauma in their family lines. Some of the common responses to trauma, especially complex trauma—that is, trauma not limited to a single incident—such as intergenerational trauma, are:

- challenges with regulating strong emotions
- a range of dissociative responses ranging from numbing to severe dissociation
- a higher incidence of tobacco, alcohol and substance use, as well as general patterns of addiction as a way to numb, manage and contain strong emotions
- autoimmune issues and chronic health conditions stemming from the somatic impact of chronic trauma responses such as hyper and hypo-arousal
- difficulties with sleep
- depression
- anxiety
- self-harm
- increased suicidality
- feelings of guilt and shame
- difficulties with trust
- lack of a felt sense of safety
- negative self-cognition
- dichotomous (all/nothing) thinking patterns
- disorganized executive functioning
- relational difficulties.

Some of these might be familiar from experiences highlighted in Chapter 2. Others might be familiar from your own history, your family of origin, your students or your clinical work.

These patterns, which are common in people as a response to trauma, especially repeated trauma over time, seem to provide some evidence that, whether epigenetics has satisfactorily proven that historical and intergenerational trauma exist or not, it is worth paying attention to intergenerational transmission of patterns, roles, stories, trauma and resilience. Since gender is a biopsychosocial construct, as well as a position in time and space, it makes sense that we learn how to do gender, what is acceptable and what is not, what can be spoken and what is best kept silent from familial patterns, as well as from larger linguistic, cultural and social patterns. After all, one could argue that familial structures are the ones that communicate the larger linguistic, cultural and social patterns from one generation to the next.

3.2 Intergenerational gendered patterns, roles and stories

I want to start from a personal story to illustrate how the stories we hear about gender and relationships can influence our views of the world, people around us and ourselves, even when these stories are not directly about us. All three of my great uncles— my grandmother's siblings—emigrated to the US after World War II. This made sense due to the economic status of Sicily after the war. I was about eight years old when the first of these great uncles died. I was really sad because he and his wife had come to visit a few years earlier. I remembered them clearly and I thought his Italo-American wife was very glamorous. As I was growing up, I also heard stories about another uncle and how, when his first wife died, there was a correspondence between him and the local "sensale,"—the mediator for a range of affairs including marriage—so that he could find a Sicilian wife who would travel to California, marry him and help him take care of his children.

I remember imagining what it would be like to be that aunt, whom I knew, and who had been too old to marry locally so was shipped off to a foreign country to marry this widow with young children, without speaking any English. This aunt never learned English and managed to communicate with anyone who spoke Spanish through a mix of Italian, English and Sicilian dialect. She eventually became a widow herself and retired back to our village in Sicily once the children had children of their own. There are more stories about relationships and migration in my family but this is a particularly formative one for me.

What does this story have to do with gender and intergenerational trauma? Let's take a moment to unpack some of the implicit messages my young self was picking up through these stories. A major one was that men got to have agency and adventure while women did not, unless they were being taken along for the ride by a man. My grandmother and her sisters did not move to the US, although my grandmother moved from Sicily to Rome with her husband and two children, which was considered its own migration. They did not seem to be as successful through my child's eyes and did not have as many opportunities as my great uncles who had migrated. Years later I would understand that their migrant experiences were fraught with xenophobia, challenges, hardship and white flight, and were not as appealing as they seemed to be to my pre-teen self.

Another implicit threat I got from the story was that if you did not marry or find a way to not be a "financial burden" to your family, you might get shipped off to a foreign country without speaking the language or having met your husband-to-be. Although this was always spoken in hushed, maybe a little disapproving, tone in my family, giving me the impression that we had different beliefs about gender and marriage, it was clearly not beyond the realm of possibilities. This, coupled with my grandmother's comments about me "ruining my eyes" through too much reading and having an "ugly cry" that I should hide from men, definitely contributed to this idea that securing a relationship needed to be a primary goal and that my value did not lie in my intellect. In fact this could even be a detriment to my erotic capital as expressed through my appearance. There are of course more stories, casual comments and messages I received not just from my family but also from the outside world, but these were pretty formative, especially when combined with the experience of living within a family unit where there was domestic violence. Once again this revolved heavily around gendered patterns of "not upsetting" my father and, for my mom, messages from other women in the family that she had "made her bed and she needed to lie in it." Divorce became a possibility in Italy in 1971, the year I was born, but the consequences for a woman's professional and social standing were still dire, should she choose to pursue a divorce.

I was absorbing not just what was being said but also what was being lived in front of me. I was picking up on underlying assumptions and I was also making up my own stories, through my child's filters and mind, as all children do. I was picking up on acceptable behaviors, and unacceptable ones, as well as on the social and familial cost that moving outside these bounds would entail. Years later I would find out much more about my family's history and realize how gendered trauma ran deep, especially the "having one's life turned upside down by relationships with men" pattern. There were also other social and cultural messages that were being passed on through my family, such as how to dress, walk and behave, and learning that whoever I was with, they would be seen as an extension and reflection of myself, my worth as a "woman" and a "wife." It would take a lot of unlearning to move away from these messages. It would also take a long time to realize that, although people in my own family had suffered because of gendered roles and expectations, they also still passed on many of these, alongside more mixed messages about being independent and "never financially, or otherwise, depend on a man," a message that funnily enough came from my abusive father.

This is just one way in which intergenerational trauma is passed on though. It would be years until I realized that the "cute birth story" my maternal grandmother was fond of telling had within it signs of how trauma had already impacted my nervous system. The story is that I came out already holding my head up and looking older than a newborn. In my 40s, through somatic work, I realized that, probably due to trauma in utero, my nervous system had come out already hypervigilant. I would also understand that my people-pleasing—also known as fawning in some trauma circles—was both validated and nurtured because of my gender assigned at birth. It was also the result of trauma and the need to monitor everyone's feelings—controlling volatility, and therefore danger, as much as possible. If trauma is the unresolved and unprocessed stories in our bodies, what are the gendered stories of our own but also of our biological parents, and their parents, and their parents before them that we carry in our bones?

Of course, we do not just carry the stories of our biological parents in our bones. If we're adopted for example, we're still deeply impacted by the stories and trauma of our adoptive parents and their familial lines, which we absorb as we grow up. I propose we look at intergenerational trauma as both being passed on through our genes and through our upbringing and yes, if this sounds complicated, it's because it is. Sometimes working with this can feel like pulling at a tangled-up ball of yarn one cannot find the beginning or end of.

In the next section I address modes of transmission, but for now I invite you to reflect on the things that we have learned both from our immediate family and caregivers, but also from stories about ancestors, as well as stories that might live in our bodies and that we might not have a well-formed or known knowledge of. What are the gender roles and gendered dynamics you witnessed growing up? What are the stories that were told again and again in your family, and the ones that were not, or were only whispered sometimes? While doing this also remember that the stories we do not know are also still living in us, so it's ok to listen to what these stories might be by tuning in somatically. Our bodies hold the stories of our ancestors. I come back to this at the end of this chapter to highlight how we hold gendered stories of survival, healing and resilience within us. For now, before focusing on modes of transmission, I want to offer you a tool to further reflect on familial patterns of gender.

Thoughtful moment: familial intergenerational patterns of gender

Take a moment to draw your family tree as far back as you can trace it. If you're familiar with genograms—a tool often used by family therapists—you might want to do that instead. If you don't have enough information to do this, please don't worry as I offer an alternative in a moment. Once you're done drawing your family tree or genogram, consider the gender roles, dynamics and stories you know about the people in your family tree or genogram. Take some time to journal about them or write some notes to remind yourself of what these roles, dynamics and stories are. Then notice whether there are connections with what you have learned about your gender, and your core assumptions about gender from the exercises in Chapter 1, as well as about your positionality and relationship with gender and community-based gendered expectations from exercises in Chapter 2. Are there connections or points of divergence?

If you do not have the information necessary to draw a family tree or genogram, take some time to listen to your body. Are there stories about gender roles, dynamic and expectations that feel familiar but maybe do not make too much sense? What are the stories that emerge when you give yourself some time to tune inwards and listen? If you have ancestral practices, you might want to ask your ancestors to share some stories with you. Whatever stories you come up with, journal or write some notes and then proceed to reflect on the questions listed above.

3.3 How is trauma passed on?

Now that we've discussed how trauma can be passed down through both epigenetic modalities (potentially) and familial narratives—spoken and unspoken—I want to turn to how trauma is passed on from generation to generation, that is, modes of transmission. As stated earlier, the transmission of gendered beliefs, ideas, roles, dynamics and messages can be implicit or explicit as well as, of course, a mixture of the two. This means that socialization, social learning and communication certainly play a major role in intergenerational trauma around rigid gender binaries. When we consider the mode of transmission, is there any more to say besides the fact that trauma is mainly passed on from generation to generation through socialization, social learning and communication?

Within families as well as within social groups and structures, Stein observed that trauma can be transmitted horizontally or vertically. Vertical transmission is from one generation to the next, while horizontal, or lateral, transmission is between members of the same family, or within a group, at the same time. Both horizontal and vertical transmission can happen at the same time. In the examples I explored in the previous section intergenerational trauma was happening both from one generation (that of my grandmother and her mother before her) to me but also laterally, or horizontally, as there was ongoing domestic violence impacting all members of the same family at the same time, albeit in different ways because of our positionality, such as parent or child. This means that as well as paying attention to social structures, socialization, social learning and communication, we might also want to notice which direction the trauma transmission is going in. If you go back to consider the notes from the thoughtful moment at the end of the previous section, for example, can you identify where there was horizontal, or lateral transmission, where the transmission was vertical and where both were/are happening at once?

Other aspects of transmission that seem worth spending some time on are related not just to the direction of the passing on of trauma but also to the quality of the transmission. For example, was the communication and learning through silence or through open and vulnerable communication about what happened? Basically, what were the patterns of the transmission process, not just the content patterns?

One of the patterns to pay attention to is dissociation.

Studies have shown that a dissociative response is common when there is what is sometimes called in the literature a betrayal trauma; that is, when the hurt is caused by someone close and who should be trustworthy, such as from a parent to a child. Childhood sexual abuse is an example of betrayal trauma and, depending on when this happened during a person's developmental course, people may or may not have any explicit memories of it, but still experience its impact. Dissociation, especially when unaddressed, can be easily passed on from a main caregiver to a child. Dissociation is a vast spectrum, which means not everyone might be aware that they have developed a dissociative response for survival. Some people, for example, might tend to over-intellectualize things, which can be a form of dissociating into prefrontal cortex thinking and not being somatically connected to one's whole self. The tendency to dissociate can be higher in people who experienced betrayal trauma in childhood and were then revictimized later on, especially by someone close to them such as an intimate partner. Dissociation is an important transmission pattern to notice because it can impact a caregiver's ability to both protect a child and to pass on healthy cues to their child, so that they can learn to identify a felt sense of safety or danger.

For example, caregivers who were abused as children and are then revictimized by an intimate partner, might develop a dissociative survival response. This might mean that they are not able to pass on to a child a healthy sense of boundaries and self-protection. When this response is coupled with patriarchal, societal structures and messages, it can lead to dissociation being viewed as valid in order to maintain the social status quo. Let's use a more concrete example: a common cis-heterosexual dominant narrative is to encourage women to dissociate in order to have sex with their male partners, even when they do not want to, as the threat is that the partner might go and "look for it elsewhere." This narrative is so common that it has been included in best-selling pop psychology self-help books such as *Mars and Venus in the Bedroom* by John Gray (2011), which was a *New York Times* bestseller. This message is also often passed on from parent to child in relation to gendered expectations around fulfilment of marital duties. If dissociation is seen as a valid survival strategy on a societal structural level for women to survive in a patriarchal system, the transmission will likely be both horizontal and vertical. Peers as well as parents and grandparents might see dissociation and crossing one's own sexual boundaries as part and parcel of making sure that the marital structure is nurtured and maintained.

Shame and blame can also play a role when considering patterns of transmission. For example, a dissociative response in order to have sex with one's husband when one does not want to, can be reinforced by the threat of social blame if the husband decides to have an affair or leave his wife. Remember what I said earlier about one's partner being viewed as an extension and reflection of the self for many people who are assigned female at birth? This means that if a man is going around in crumpled clothes or has an affair, in some cis-heterosexual, patriarchal dominant narratives, his wife would somehow be to blame for this.

Blame and shame are powerful tools of social learning and social policing. This is often how the status quo is maintained and how we learn not to wander too far away from the path of normativity. For example, trans, nonbinary and gender expansive children learn very early on what is acceptable and what is not through shame and blame. In one of the first season's episodes of the popular Netflix series *Pose*—"Giving and Receiving"—one of the main characters, Angel, a trans woman, talks about an episode that impacted her feelings about Christmas. She was very young when she saw a pair of red pumps. They were so beautiful and all that she wanted for Christmas. However, even at four or five years old, she knew she needed to keep this desire silent, so she stole one of the shoes. When they got home, she tried to run upstairs but the shoe fell from the coat and Angel recalls how her father slapped her across the face, in her words "for stealing, but more so for what I chose to steal." In this brief moment in the episode and in these few words so much is communicated about gender and how cisgenderism and transphobia are upheld through familial dynamics. Angel goes on to say that her father never looked at her in the same way since. Nothing was directly spoken about gender but the action and the silence not only shamed Angel but also blamed her for having a desire she "should" not have according to familial, social and cultural structures and expectations.

Dissociation, silence, blame and shame are powerful modalities often involved in both horizontal and vertical trauma transmission. All these modalities are needed to uphold not only an inequitable but also a contracted experience of gender in our individual and collective soma. Toxic masculinity demands dissociation from emotions and emotional needs and expressions for masculine people, such as crying, expressing sadness and vulnerability, or needing healthy touch, emotional intimacy and tenderness. Toxic masculinity also demands dissociation from feminine people, dissociation from healthy boundaries, from the mobilization of anger and healthy fight responses, and from other feminine people who, in this context, need to be viewed as competition rather than as people who are laterally impacted by the same trauma of a patriarchal view of gender.

Gender normativity is also often upheld in silence. Sometimes gender norms are explicitly named but most often they're passed on through much more subtle cues, as in the *Pose* episode mentioned earlier, such as gaze, social isolation or exclusion and so on. Blame and shame are then the tools used to police any deviation from gender normativity, be these deviations of identity (such as for the character of Angel in *Pose*) of role (such as a feminine person choosing to prioritize career over relationships) or expression (such as people of any gender identity not conforming to scripted societal expectations, but especially anyone assigned male at birth donning any kind of feminine apparel from skirts, to jewellery or make up, depending on their cultural context).

Intergenerational gendered trauma and the way it is passed on also impacts the ways in which we might show up in relationships, from collegial relationships to friendships and especially in intimate partnerships. If we were to adopt views from attachment theory, we could say that these factors contribute to our attachment style, which strongly influences—and according to some determines—the way we do relationships. This is something that I address more closely in the next chapter since relationships are such a vast topic they deserve more space than just a section. Before addressing relationships though, I want to spend a moment reflecting on the role of power, blame and shame in a rigid gender binary as trauma and then considering the importance of ancestral connection as an antidote to intergenerational trauma.

Educational stretch: the role of
power, blame and shame

Take a moment to review your core assumptions about gender,
the gendered expectations in your communities and the intergenerational patterns of gender identified through the "Thoughtful
moment" activity at the end of the previous section. You may
even want to start compiling them altogether, almost creating
a gender map. If you work somatically you might want to take
some time to use a body outline (maybe even draw an outline
of your own body on a large piece of paper) and consider where
these assumptions, expectations and patterns live in your body.
Once you feel you have a good map, body map or even a mental
landscape of these, ask yourself the following questions:

1. Where do these assumptions, expectations and patterns
   of gender come from? Did I learn/deduce these from
   people who had authority over me, either because of
   age and/or age + role (such as parents, grandparents,
   teachers, spiritual leaders, camp counselors and so on)?
   Did they come from ancestral stories? If so, how were
   these passed on?

2. Is there blame, shame or both present in these assumptions, expectations and patterns? If so, how do these
   manifest? Did anyone communicate a sense of shame
   and/or blame to me, or did I deduce it from other people's actions, silences or comments about other people?

3. Are there places where I feel other people have power
   over my current assumptions, expectations and patterns
   of gender? If so, what are those places and who are

the people and/or structures who have power over my current views?

4. Are there places where I experience blame or shame about my current assumptions, expectations and patterns of gender? If so, what are those places and where does the blame or shame come from? What do blame or shame in these areas open up or close down?

5. Are there places where I, implicitly or explicitly, communicate blame or shame about other people's assumptions, expectations and patterns of gender? If so, what are those places and why do I feel the need to communicate blame or shame in these areas? Do I have power over the people to whom I am communicating blame or shame in these areas? If so how might power impact the messages I am communicating about other people's assumptions, expectations and patterns of gender?

Take some time to map the answers to these questions on to your initial map. If you're using a physical, written out or drawn map, you may want to use different colors, shapes or images to represent different experiences. If you notice your body contracting, such as your shoulders rising or your neck tightening or your breathing becoming shallow, slow down and pay attention to your body. What is it that you need to do to take care of yourself in this moment? This can be challenging work and I encourage you to go slow, breathe and take the time you need to engage with these ideas. If you're finding yourself activated and/or contracted, take a break from the book, try to move your body within your capacity, listen to some music that helps you reconnect with a felt sense of safety and wellbeing in your body, talk to a trusted friend, have a cup of tea or take a bath or shower. Sometimes a state change can be very helpful in supporting nervous system regulation. When you're once more regulated, relaxed, yet also alert and ready to learn, this book will still be here waiting for you.

3.4 The importance of ancestral connections

I mentioned earlier in this chapter that some people believe that, as well as trauma, we can inherit healing wisdom, resilience, creativity and strength from our ancestors. This means that, in addition to intergenerational trauma, we can experience intergenerational resilience. I want to acknowledge that the idea of intergenerational resilience is rooted in Indigenous knowledge and that much of what I address in this section comes indeed from either Indigenous paradigms and/or Black and Latinx scholarship and writing. If a rigid gender binary is indeed a structural, social and intergenerational trauma, as I am posing in this book, and also part of the historical trauma of settler colonialism, then part of its antidote and remedy needs to be rooted in Indigenous knowledge and practices. At some point in our ancestral lines there are people who were Indigenous to place, who knew what it was like to be connected to a place, a language, a collective soma. I do not want to romanticize the past. None of our ancestors are perfect, whether Indigenous or not. I do not want to go in search of a romantic connected past; I'm interested in nurturing the idea of a connected present.

If part of the trauma and legacy of settler colonialism is displacement, in a range of ways depending on our own positionality, then connection is part of the remedy. As humans we need connection and this is now well documented in interpersonal neurobiological research and clinical practices. Part of our connection is connection to time, to our place in time, to the past and to lineage. Many of us might not be able to trace our own ancestral lineages but the popularity of commercial enterprises such as ancestry.com and 23andme seems to document a hunger for connection in our collective soma. Connecting to ancestors past the immediate ones we might have known during our lifetime, such as parents or grandparents, aunts and uncles, and so on can be powerful, especially if the ancestors we have known when alive were abusive and/or rejecting of who we are. Somewhere in our lines there are ancestors who love us just as we are, no matter what our gender identities, roles, expressions or experiences might be. Somewhere in our lines, maybe not our bloodlines but our lines of activism or spirituality or culture, there are gender blessed ancestors[1] who have maybe found ways to expand their own views and other people's views and experiences of gender. Connecting to those ancestors can be a source of psychological, emotional, cultural and spiritual wellbeing for many of us. However, ancestral connection and practices are not often considered part of mainstream psychological or therapeutic approaches given that these are rooted, by and large, within Anglo, white-dominated, settler colonial contexts.

When I first started to acknowledge ancestors when teaching as well as bringing up ancestors in therapeutic work, I felt deeply uncomfortable, despite having grown up with ancestral practices, especially from the maternal Sicilian line of my mother

---

1   I want to attribute, acknowledge and thank Dr Pavini Moray, host of the podcast Bespoken Bones and somatic practitioner, for the term "gender blessed ancestors."

and grandmother. Somehow to do this in an Anglo context felt like deviating from the normative part of separating personal from public, spiritual from psychological, yet I also found it to be powerful for the spaces I created and for the possibilities it opened up for both learners and clients. On a more personal note I have experienced the strength and healing it brought me as a trans masculine, nonbinary, queer person to connect with blood, culture and spirit lineages of more gender expansive people, including healing and movement practitioners. As an educator, supervisor and clinician, being able to talk about gender expansive ancestors opens up possibilities beyond the more medicalized and pathologizing current Western-dominant paradigm.

If you're not spiritual or religious, or have maybe experienced spiritual or religious trauma, and are getting nervous, uncomfortable or even angry about this section, please note that I do not believe that connection with ancestors is purely a spiritual practice. If you've ever connected with, or felt moved and inspired by, a story written by or about dead people, you have experienced a connection with ancestors. While I do connect to ancestors through spiritual practices, we can also connect with ancestors through stories, oral and written. Honoring ancestors is about having a sense of connection to time, knowing we're not the first to have experienced something or to have felt a certain way, and that what we do has an impact on those who come after us, not just in terms of our bloodline but also just those who will continue living when we're dead.

What do ancestors have to do with gendered intergenerational trauma though? If many of our more contracted views, experiences and expressions of gender have been passed on intergenerationally, including through dissociative responses, shame and blame, then turning towards the ancestors to learn more expansive or even just different views, experiences and expressions of gender can be powerful.

One of the most frequent questions asked by trans and/or nonbinary clients and their spouses and families, especially when they're struggling with acceptance, is why they are the way they are. I also don't believe that it's just trans, nonbinary and gender expansive clients who ask themselves that question. As humans we often need to be able to tell a story about what we're experiencing, to make meaning out of it. If we feel we're deviating from the gender normative path in any way at all, whether it is by choosing to not have children as a woman, to be tender and vulnerable as a man, or to enjoy activities that gendered expectations would have us believe are "wrong," we need to make some sense of it. I believe that ancestral connection, whether through spirit, historical knowledge or storytelling, can make us feel less alone, less "other" and can, therefore, be a remedy, an antidote to blame and shame. What does it mean to connect with ancestors or help our students, patients or clients connect to ancestors in practice? Let's take a look at a clinical vignette to explore this further.

Clinical vignette: gender blessed ancestors as a source of resilience and healing

"Dean is in his 30s and would like to have a child but is not in a relationship. He has always wanted to be a father but has not yet found a person he wants to marry or co-parent with. Dean has been thinking about adopting but has run into a fair deal of stigma from adoption agencies and social workers. As a man he is seen as suspect in his desire to nurture and raise a child. Dean feels isolated from family and friends who don't understand why he doesn't just 'marry someone' so that he can have a child in the way that's 'expected' of him. He has been starting to wonder whether there is 'something wrong' with him for having this desire and this has brought him to therapy to address this further."

Take a moment to notice what assumptions you may be making about who Dean is. For example, what do you imagine his gender identity and sexuality to be? What about his race and/or ethnicity, his class and economic status, his disability status, or relationship to Indigeneity? What are the first thoughts, reactions and emotions that come up for you when you read this case study? What are the questions you would move towards? What are you curious about? Try to notice the answer to these questions with as much curiosity, self-compassion and lack of self-judgement as you can muster in this moment. This is just information. We're all impacted by dominant ideas that may or may not be in line with our values. Whatever your answers might be, try to let them be what they are.

Once you have considered these questions, take a moment to consider how you would approach this therapeutically. There are, of course, many ways to approach working with Dean but in this vignette I want to offer the possibility of working with ancestors. For example, you could do a genogram with Dean and then explore this with him through the lens of parenting. What are the beliefs about parenting that he has learned from his family and his family's stories? Does his desire really deviate from how parenting happens in his family? If so, is it possible that at some point, someone in the world has had the same desire? This does not need to be an ancestor of blood; it could be an author who has written about this, or just a person who has parented a child alone even though they were a man.

Explore what impact it has for Dean to consider that he is not the first person in the world to have this desire. In fact, you may even encourage Dean to do some research about single fathers by choice. What can open up for Dean if he considers that somewhere in the past there has been a man, just like him, who felt tenderness and a strong desire to be a parent, to raise a child, not just because he was in a relationship but because that's what he wanted?

You might even want to encourage Dean to imagine he can communicate with this gender blessed ancestor who shared this desire and/or experience to be a father, even though he was not in a relationship. You could ask Dean what this ancestor would say to him if he were in the therapy room with them. Or you could ask Dean to write a letter to this ancestor. You could invite Dean to have tea with this ancestor and ask him some questions, if Dean is spiritually inclined. There might even be a ritual in therapy about supporting Dean in imagining that he is part of a long line of men across time and space who have felt the desire to be fathers, and who prize the nurturing and raising of children. This ritual could be a guided meditation, or making a collage, or a somatic exploration of a felt sense of belonging and connection. You, and/or your clients, may, of course, already have ways of bringing ancestral connection into your clinical work. If so, you may want to apply your ideas, frameworks and interventions to this case.

Summary

In the next chapter I address the impact of everything we have talked about on gendered dynamics in relationships. First, here are the main points addressed in this chapter.

- The main distinction between historical and intergenerational trauma is that the former is collective, and it involves a large number of people and specific historical events, beyond an individual family line.
- One of the reasons why we're looking at the complexity of a rigid gender binary as trauma is that it's not only transmitted through larger historical and social patterns, but also in the everyday interactions we experience from day one of our lives, and some researches would say even in utero.
- The field of epigenetics, in particular, has attempted to document how historical and intergenerational trauma is not just passed on from parent to child through behaviors and relationships, but also through our genes.
- The term transgenerational indicates the passing on of trauma from one generation to the next; once we consider effects in the third generation and beyond, the term intergenerational is generally used.
- Dr. Degruy-Leary (1994) identified a phenomenon they called Post-Traumatic Slave Syndrome (PTSS) to indicate the psychological and emotional trauma from slavery. PTSS clearly delineates how the past has an ongoing impact on the present for Black people in the US.
- We do not just carry the stories of our biological parents in our bones. If we're adopted for example, we're still

deeply impacted by the stories and trauma of our adoptive parents and their familial lines, which we absorb as we grow up.

- The transmission of gendered beliefs, ideas, roles, dynamics and messages can be implicit or explicit as well as, of course, a mixture of the two.
- Trauma can be transmitted horizontally or vertically. Vertical transmission is from one generation to the next, while horizontal, or lateral, transmission is between members of the same family, or within a group, at the same time. Both horizontal and vertical transmission can happen at the same time.
- Dissociation is an important transmission pattern to notice because it can impact a caregiver's ability to both protect a child and to pass on healthy cues to their child, so that they can learn to identify a felt sense of safety or danger.
- A common cis-heterosexual dominant narrative is to encourage women to dissociate in order to have sex with their male partners even when they do not want to, or the partner will go and "look for it elsewhere."
- If dissociation is seen as a valid survival strategy on a societal structural level for women to survive in a patriarchal system, the transmission will likely be both horizontal and vertical.
- Toxic masculinity demands dissociation from emotions and emotional needs and expressions for masculine people, such as crying, expressing sadness and vulnerability, or needing healthy touch, emotional intimacy and tenderness.
- As well as intergenerational trauma, we can experience

intergenerational resilience. The idea of intergenerational resilience is rooted in Indigenous knowledge, and has also been explored by Black and Latinx scholars and writers.

- If a rigid gender binary is a structural, social and intergenerational trauma, and an aspect of the historical trauma of settler colonialism, then part of its antidote and remedy needs to be rooted in Indigenous knowledge and practices.
- If part of the trauma and legacy of settler colonialism is displacement, in a range of ways depending on our own positionality, then connection, including ancestral connection, is part of the remedy.

CHAPTER 4

Relationships

In the previous chapter I explored what epigenetics is and whether it might have a role to play when it comes to gender as trauma. I also highlighted how gendered stories, patterns and roles are passed on from one generation to the next, including a discussion of the role of ancestral connections in individual and collective resilience.

Much of the discussion in the previous chapter, as well as in this book, focuses on the relational nature of trauma. Gender is not something that exists purely on an individualized level but rather something that happens between us and within historical, cultural and social contexts.

In this chapter, I focus more closely on relationships, and especially, but not exclusively, romantic and sexual relationships. First, I address how the way we conceptualize gender in dominant culture influences our relationships and might lead to unhealthy relational patterns and dynamics. Then I discuss how toxic rigid gender binaries, such as toxic masculinity, might manifest and be upheld in relationships. This leads into considering intimate partner violence and its roots in these toxic gendered stories, patterns and roles. At the end of the chapter, I explore the larger systemic cultural context of rape culture within which sexual gendered violence emerges and thrives.

4.1 The influence of dominant ideas of gender on relationships

In section 3.3, I discuss some examples of how gendered trauma can be passed on both horizontally and vertically. One of the examples referred to is John Gray's advice in *Mars and Venus in the Bedroom* (2011), in which he encourages women to think of something else when they have sex with their husband in order to avoid their husbands looking for sex "elsewhere." This piece of advice is congruent with some dominant ideas about gender and relationship, such as that women/femme people are responsible for the sexual needs of men/masculine people. It is also something that it is often reinforced both vertically, from one generation to the next, and horizontally, from peer to peer.

This idea is rooted in how sexuality is conceptualized through the lens of (cis)gender. Let's take a moment to break this idea down in some of its main components.

Women

In many dominant Western/Global North cultures, women are taught in a myriad of ways to view their sexuality through the male gaze. This means that their desirability is based on whether men find them attractive and desirable. Growing up, for example, my grandmother would often comment that I was "ruining" my eyes through "too much reading," warning me that this would make me less "desirable" to prospective husbands. She was referring to needing glasses as something that would reduce my erotic capital, that is, my level of attractiveness based on the perception of others, usually men. She was also suggesting that reading too much was something that would make me less desirable as it might lead me to be better educated than a prospective husband. This idea of feminine desirability and attractiveness being based in the masculine gaze is referred to, in social philosophy and psychology, as objectification.

Objectification theory, in this context, offers a framework to understand how girls and women are often acculturated to view themselves as objects offered to, and evaluated through, the male gaze and its values. Objectification is therefore dehumanizing and, within this framework, women and feminine people are encouraged to constantly self-monitor through an internalized other. This can lead to decreased capacity for interoception: that is, the ability to know our internal states. This is linked to disordered eating, loss of sexual agency and many negative mental health outcomes for women. Objectification is also congruent with the advice by John Gray to women where he encourages them to meet their (male) partners' needs with little to no regard to their own self-consent, desire or pleasure. Within this framework, feminine sexualities exist to meet the needs of masculine sexualities and not as autonomous agents of desire, pleasure and consent.

Men

Objectification of girls and women also impacts boys and men and, to a degree, dehumanizes their sexuality as well. In this framework, male sexuality is usually viewed as "animalistic," unbridled and always "up for it." Men are not viewed as autonomous agents either but rather as out of control and driven by their sexual needs above all others. This leaves no space for men/masculine people who are asexual, demisexual or have low libido due to a range of factors. It also places men and masculine people firmly as "aggressors" and "dominant" in sexual relationships, which, as I examine later in this chapter, is problematic on multiple levels as well as being dehumanizing. In this framework the sexual and relational script for all genders is extremely narrow and not conducive to authentic rapport and communication.

Marginalized genders and sexualities

This framework does not impact only cishetero men and women. It also impacts people with marginalized gender and sexual identities, since we are all acculturated to monitor ourselves against normative beauty standards, which are usually set within patriarchal, white supremacist, classist and ableist lenses. This means that, for example, queer men are also impacted by issues such as disordered eating, especially when experiencing high levels of internalized queerphobia. Trans and nonbinary people are also not immune to these dominant ideals of beauty, desirability, sexuality and relationships. For example, we might try to pass—that is, to be viewed as cis—by meeting normative standards of appearance, not because this is a genuine desire or just because it is safer, but because there seem to be no other possibilities to exist as our own authentic selves.

Once more we cannot view gender as separate from other aspects of our identities and experiences. This means that queer relationships and sexualities are also impacted by dominant ideas of gender. This can be clearly seen in some of the homonormative examples of coupledom in popular media, such as Mitch and Cam in *Modern Family*, where gender (and queer) stereotypes are played out in a range of ways. Both Mitch and Cam are often portrayed as being very attentive to their appearance, as well as being viewed as divas who value other people's perceptions of them. This and other similar portrayals align queer male sexuality with femininity, just as queer female sexuality is often viewed as closer to masculinity, such as in the characters of Alex Danvers and Maggie Sawyer in *Supergirl*, who both work in traditionally male-dominated professions.

If gender is conceptualized as binary, and so is sexuality, then it makes sense that queer sexuality would be overimposed on this blueprint, reinforcing another dominant stereotype that "love is love" regardless of the gender of the people involved in the relationship, and that understanding this is enough for equality to become a reality.

However, the reality is that the gender of the people involved in the relationship actually matters a great deal, not just in television shows but in everyday life. For example, queer sexualities are often viewed as "less than," especially in relation to women, trans and nonbinary people when no cis male gaze is involved, thereby demoting the validity of these identities or relationships. For example, let's take a moment to consider things like "one penis policies" in polyamorous and other ethically nonmonogamous circles. The one penis policy is exactly what it seems to be: only one penis is allowed in the relationship. Underlying implications are that only another penis could be a possible threat to the established relationship. This not only automatically demotes any queer sexuality that does not include a cis man to lesser than cishetero couplings but it's also transphobic, given that it is rooted in gender essentialism, within which anatomy is viewed as inherently gendered. This kind of policy is also often biphobic as it implies that bisexuality in women and femmes is in service, and subservient to, male gaze and desire, another common trope in dominant culture.

Disability

Queerness is not the only aspect of identity and experience that interacts with dominant ideas of gender in relationships. Being disabled also influences the ways in which objectification is enacted in dominant culture. Given that part of femininity within this framework is to be objectified for the male gaze and pleasure and that part of masculinity is to be aggressive and always ready to be sexual, disability is often viewed, in dominant culture, as nonsexual. The combination of objectification and the dominant idea that sexuality is only the domain of young and middle adulthood means that usually disabled people are infantilized within the overculture. Disabled people are often viewed as vulnerable, and therefore potential sexual victims, or as having "perverse/deviant" sexualities. These images are not uncommon in media representations of disabled people and are consistent with polarized portrayals of disabled people as either "angels," rising above adversity, or as "villains," embittered by their disabilities.

These portrayals are often conflated with gender, with disabled (usually white) women more likely to be viewed as innocent and/or victims and disabled (especially Black) men more likely to be viewed as dangerous villains. In everyday life, dominant discourses and popular media the sexuality of disabled people is then invisible, unspoken and unspeakable, with disabled bodies being viewed as having no erotic capital within a mainstream gaze. When disabled people are also gender expansive, trans and/or nonbinary, queer, kinky or nonmonogamous, we are often viewed as deviating from normative discourses of gender and sexuality because of our disabilities, rather than our identities and experiences being considered legitimate. This then reinforces narrow ideas of what constitutes good and legitimate sexual expressions. If disabled people are viewed as taking refuge in identities and practices that are viewed as "other", because mainstream identities and behaviors are precluded to them, then those identities and practices are also implicitly being defined as not only "other" but also "lesser than" mainstream identities and behaviours. This creates a cycle of continually placing outside the boundaries of "normality" identities and behaviours that are seen as "deviant:" only people who are viewed as being somewhat lesser in mainstream society would identify with and engage in behaviors that are also seen as lesser.

Race

Racialized identities and dynamics are also essential to consider when discussing dominant ideas of gender in relationships, as discussed in the previous chapters. Dominant discourses of gender are also colonial, white dominant discourses. This means that bodies are not only racialized in dominant discourses but also sexualized and gendered upon the foundations of settler colonialism and white supremacy. For example, Black male sexuality is often viewed as dangerous, aggressive, irresponsible and predatory towards white women, an incredibly dangerous trope that has led to the incarceration and murder of too many Black men. Black women's sexuality is not only viewed through a male gaze but through a cis white male gaze and is often portrayed as hypersexualized in comparison to the sexuality of white women. Where the latter are viewed through the Madonna/whore lens, in dominant discourse Black women's sexuality can only exist through the whore half of that lens. The hypersexualization of

Black, Brown and Indigenous bodies also impacts the level of violence experienced by these bodies, as addressed later in this chapter and in previous chapters.

Other stereotypes and dangerous tropes where gender and racialized identities meet include that of subservient, hyper-feminine and docile Asian women as well as Asian masculinity being viewed as more "feminine" and/or androgynous than white masculinity. I have also already mentioned, in Chapter 2, the incredibly damaging tropes of Indigenous men as "ineffective and lazy" and of women as "sexually loose, mercenary, and innately immoral," and how the legacy of these tropes is still evident in the exploitation experienced by Indigenous girls, women and LGBTQ2 people who are often viewed as targets for commercial sexual exploitation.

Objectification and ownership

It is impossible, therefore, to talk about dominant discourses around gender in relationships without addressing all these other aspects of identities and experiences. A thread that runs through all these aspects is how objectification is also inter-woven with the idea of ownership. If women and femininity exist for and are dependent on the male gaze, the latter is then inherently superior and agentic. The agency of the male gaze is then often expressed through the implication of ownership. Common expressions such as "my girl" imply that ownership is not only possible but even desirable in relationships. If the goal is to be attractive and desirable to the male gaze and to serve masculine sexualities, then ownership can be viewed as the ultimate public declaration of erotic capital and becomes a substitute for the very human desire to belong.

Before moving forward, however, I want to emphasize that I

am not talking about the consensual and negotiated ownership that is characteristic of some 24/7 BDSM relational dynamics, but rather about the implicit, assumed ownership that arises from objectification. I address how the constructs of gender and ownership are woven more firmly together through social institutions such as marriage in Chapter 5. For now, suffice to say that the idea of ownership in relation to gender is particularly prominent in how the relationship between fathers and daughters is viewed in dominant discourse. This is evident in popular Internet memes focusing on fathers' views around their daughters dating, such as in images and t-shirts about "rules for dating my daughters." One of the more popular images lists the following rules:

1. Get a job
2. Understand I don't like you
3. I'm everywhere
4. You hurt her, I hurt you
5. Be home early
6. Don't lie to me, I will find out
7. Get a lawyer
8. She's my angel, not your conquest
9. I don't mind going back to the jail
10. Whatever you do to her, I do to you.

These "rules" imply both ownership by the father and lack of agency for daughters and include several aspects of toxic masculinity, which I unpack in the following section. There are no equivalent "rules" for fathers of boys, reinforcing the idea that girls are supposed to be "passed on" from fathers to husbands as passive recipients of "benevolent" protection. Before we move on to the next section though, let's take a moment to reflect further on the content discussed so far.

Thoughtful moment: what we learn about gender from the relationships around us

You have already been invited to reflect on what you have learned about gender in history and to reflect on your own relationship to gender and your family's gender history. Now, I invite you once more to pause and reflect on what you have learned about gender from the relationships around you. Below I offer a format to guide you but feel free to do this in a way that makes sense to you.

Take a moment to pick a relationship that you were exposed to frequently growing up; this could be your parents, one of your parents/caregivers and a grandparent or sibling, a teacher and their classroom, or a spiritual leader and their faith community. Then take a moment to pick a relationship that you came into frequent contact with in your early adulthood and finally a relationship that you know well in this stage of your life. These relationships can be chosen from your own life, or from books, movies or TV characters.

Now reflect on what you have learned about gender dynamics in relationships from each of these three contexts. What did you observe? What sense did you make of these observations? What were some of the implicit gender messages in these relationships? Were the gender dynamics in these relationships congruent with your own identities, experiences and understanding of gender? If so, in what ways? If not, why not? What were/ are the differences? If you want, you can write your reflections down or record them in a voice memo so you can come back to them later.

4.2 Toxic gender binaries in relationships

I mentioned in the previous section of this chapter that the idea of parenting as ownership is rooted both in sexual objectification and toxic masculinity. In this section I take some time to explore this further, as well as to define what toxic masculinity and, more generally, toxic cisgenderism are, how they show up in everyday dominant culture, and how they impact our relationships. The "rules for dating my daughter" memes and images that I mentioned earlier are but the tip of the iceberg when it comes to parenting and ownership within a toxic, compulsive, cisheteronormative framework. Let's examine this a little more closely.

First of all, let's separate the idea of ownership from belonging. Children do need to experience belonging and unconditional love. These are essential to our growth and wellbeing when we come into the world and, if we're deprived of these, then we experience developmental trauma, given that some of our basic needs were not met. Ownership, on the other hand, is not about belonging but rather about property, which goes along well with objectification. To own someone is to somehow dehumanize them and deprive them of agency.

Parenting
Historically, as I address in the next chapter, we can see this manifest in women's assets being owned by their fathers, husbands or other male relatives in certain cultures and within specific

timelines. One of the ways in which parents assert ownership over their children is branding their gender on the basis of visible genitalia and sex assigned at birth. This branding is even socially celebrated through gender reveal parties, which have become popular enough in mainstream US culture to be depicted on the award-winning show *This Is Us*, and then reinforced through gendered baby clothing, toys, celebratory balloons and so on.

As well as often determining their children's gender identities at, or even before, birth, parents are usually encouraged in dominant culture to view children as an extension of themselves, including their own gendered expectations. I remember taking part in focus groups when my child was a baby, where other mothers (and yes, it was a group of just mothers) were gushing over how happy they were to be able to "dress up their little girls" and how disappointed those who only had boys were that this experience was "denied" to them.

As children grow up, there starts to be an even starker divide, with boys being encouraged to become more independent and have adventures, while girls are seen as property to be protected from other people's predatory boys. In the US there are even purity balls, the sole purpose of which is to promote virginity amongst girls. These balls are usually attended by girls who are accompanied by their fathers who pledge themselves as protectors of their daughters' "purity." Of course, purity in this context is viewed as equivalent to virginity. If girls' and women's erotic capital is dependent upon the male gaze, their value is placed on being seen as a desirable property to be acquired by "the right man at the right time." In the meantime, girls' purity is under the custody and protection of their fathers. It's hard not to see purity balls, in which fathers are described as dates and even encouraged to praise their daughters' physical beauty, as a form of grooming for patriarchal, compulsive cisheteonormative practices.

Toxic masculinity

These types of interactions are also founded on a construct that is often referred to as toxic masculinity. In the case of purity balls or the "ten rules to date my daughter" memes, toxic masculinity and ownership are barely hidden underneath the veneer of moral respectability and the excuse of protection. Toxic masculinity is not inherent to being a man/masculine person but rather it indicates a set of norms contributing to a cultural mindset that perpetuates harmful stereotypes and rigid gender binaries. Seemingly simple and innocent expressions like "boys will be boys" are part of toxic masculinity and are rooted in gender essentialism and biological determinism, which I discussed in Chapter 1. When we say things like "let boys be boys" or "boys don't cry," we dehumanize boys and men by asking them to fit into a narrow script of gender where strength is equated with lack of emotional expression and high tolerance for (and little to no protection from) pain and violence, and sexuality becomes legitimate only if dominant within a cisheteronormative dynamic.

Within a framework of toxic masculinity, certain topics, tasks and areas are viewed as the inherent domain of men. Expressions such as "mansplaining" stem in fact from the assumption that a man would automatically know better on any given subject, especially if that subject is stereotypically viewed as "masculine," such as science, engineering, mechanics, weightlifting and so on. Within a framework of toxic masculinity, we also assume that men should be breadwinners and protectors and that to not live up to these ideals is emasculating, which is, within this value system, one of the worst things that can happen to a man.

Toxic masculinity is not automatically and only upheld by men. While men are encouraged to adhere to toxic masculine ideals in dominant culture, all of us are invited into the dance of toxic masculinity through societal scripts. For example, toxic masculinity also thrives on ideas of femininity as inherently weak and in need of help and support. This means that when girls and women are using their erotic capital to get out of getting a speeding ticket or to cover up mistakes at work by saying they didn't understand something, they are also playing into the same patriarchal framework of toxic masculinity. It might appear at first glance that these behaviors could be grouped under the umbrella of toxic femininity. However, the salient difference between toxic masculinity and toxic femininity is that while the former glorifies dominance, the latter seems to be all about subservience to male dominance and supposedly inherent superiority. This means that rather than talking about toxic femininity, which seems to be a false equivalence, we might be better served by recognizing how toxic masculinity thrives in the soil of toxic cisgenderism and how it can be upheld by people of all genders.

Toxic cisgenderism

Toxic cisgenderism, and I would argue that all cisgenderism is toxic, is not inherent to cis people but rather it's a "prejudicial ideology" that assumes cisgender identities and experiences as inherently natural, desirable, and as such superior to, any other gender identities and experiences. Cisgenderism is also rooted in gender essentialism and biological determinism.

Cisgenderism starts early in dominant culture, given that our genders are usually presumed to be cis until proven otherwise. It is then reinforced through parenting, education and many other systems, as examined in the next chapter. Cisgenderism contributes greatly to the reproduction of toxic, rigid gender binaries within relationships, including the examples around parenting given so far. Cisgenderism also interacts with all other aspects of our identities and expressions. For example, it is far safer for white people to express their gender in more expansive ways, whereas Black, Brown and Indigenous bodies are more closely scrutinized, policed and punished for transgressing gender norms, as highlighted in previous chapters. Ableism also intersects with cisgenderism as any deviation from cisgenderism can be viewed as a response to being disabled rather than as an authentic identity and/or expression.

Attraction

Relationally these rigid binaries are also mirrored in the narrow confines within which rapport can occur. Whether it's purity balls or toxic masculinity in general, a rigid gender binary is usually only conducive to either heternormative or homonormative relationships as these relationships do not undermine its foundations. Interracial and interabled relationships are also often challenging within this framework due to the entwined nature of cisgenderism with white supremacy and ableism. In fact, research studies have found that the combination of racial and gender stereotypes might even influence who we find attractive. For example, a US-based study found that if a man is strongly attracted to femininity, he is more likely to be attracted to Asian women and less so to Black women, given the dominant cultural stereotypes of the former as feminine and docile and the latter as strong and aggressive. On the other hand, women attracted to masculinity were more likely to be attracted to Black men and less so to Asian men, given the gender stereotypes associated with these racialized identities. Class also comes into play when considering relational patterns, with women being more likely to be attracted to men with higher status and men being less likely to be attracted to women with higher status than theirs and more likely to choose partners of a lower socioeconomic status.

While some of these studies are steeped in biological determinism and view who we are attracted to as a facet of evolutionary reproduction, others would argue that dominant cultural discourses and systemic oppression influence who we find attractive and partner with. Those influences are deeply rooted in cisgenderism, white supremacy, racism, classism, ableism and in the ongoing settler colonial project as discussed in Chapter 1.

Basically our attraction to others, the way in which we judge our own level of attractiveness and desirability, as well as our relationships are shaped by historical, cultural and social trauma. This means that part of our work as providers, educators and/ or researchers is to know this so that we, at the very least, do not continue to perpetuate the same harmful stereotypes and relational dynamics. As discussed in the next section, this is not only an intellectual exercise but rather a potentially life-saving one as certain bodies are deeply impacted by systemic violence through their relationships with partners, parents and broader systems, such as education and healthcare, which I explore in Chapter 5. Before I go on to illustrate how some harmful dynamics can be perpetuated in intimate partner relationships though, I want to take a moment to consider how the ideas discussed so far might be applied within a clinical framework.

Clinical vignette: navigating teenage dating

The following is not an uncommon scenario for both families and sex therapists alike.

"Sam is 16 years old and their parents found them sexting with the person they have been dating for the past few months. Sam doesn't think there's anything wrong with what they're doing and feels their parents are 'freaking out over nothing.' Sam's parents are concerned about the impact this will have on their future if any of the texts and pictures are made public. They also feel that Sam is too young to date or be involved in any sort of sexual relationship."

Take a moment, as you did in the previous chapter, to notice what assumptions you might be making about Sam and their parents. What gender, sexuality, race/ethnicity and class do you imagine them to be? What about spirituality and/or religion, if any? What beliefs do you think Sam and their parents might hold with regards to sex, and what do you think these beliefs might be based on? What are the first thoughts, reactions and emotions that come up for you when you read this case study? How do you think your own beliefs and experiences might impact the way you view this case? As stated in the last chapter, try to notice the answer to these questions with as much curiosity, self-compassion and lack of self-judgement as you are capable of in this moment. This is just information. We're all impacted by dominant ideas that may or may not be in line with our values. Whatever your answers might be, try to let them be what they are.

Now, think about how you would approach this therapeutically. What questions would you ask and to whom? How would you address the family system? Would you work with Sam and their parents separately or together? What would influence your choice? What would your agenda be both with regards to Sam and their parents? Would you have a goal in mind? If so, what would your goal be based on? If you have thought of a gender and/or other aspects of identity and experiences for Sam, how do these imagined identities and experiences impact your therapeutic approach, if at all? Would your approach change if you were to assign to Sam different identities? What about Sam's partner? Or Sam's parents? What do you imagine their identities to be? How does this influence the way you might view their interaction? If you assign a different identity to Sam's partner, to Sam or to Sam's parents, does that change the way in which you would approach this case therapeutically?

Finally, I invite you to consider how the concepts discussed in this chapter so far might be applicable to this vignette. How might dominant discourses of gender impact the way in which you are considering this case? How might they impact Sam's attitude towards their behavior and their parents' reaction? How might dominant discourses of gender influence Sam's parents in this situation? What would your therapeutic role be in this situation? Is your role in harmony with dominant discourses of gender or not? If not, how does it differ? How is your role as a provider impacted by dominant discourses of gender in this situation, as well as in your overall practice? You may already have thought through these issues in your own practice of course.

4.3 Intimate partner violence

I mentioned towards the end of the previous section that some bodies are more impacted than others by systemic power dynamics and oppression and the way in which they manifest in our relationships. In this section, I want to take some time to address intimate partner violence more explicitly for a number of reasons. First, intimate partner violence is far too common and is responsible for nearly half the number of women killed by homicide in the United States. Second, despite being described as a public health concern by agencies such as the CDC (Center for Disease Control) in the US, many educators and therapists do not receive enough training on how to address intimate partner violence, and especially teen dating violence, which is also more common than you might be aware of. Finally, as a child survivor of violence, witness to intimate partner violence growing up and then as an adult survivor of intimate partner violence, I am personally invested in making sure that this topic is addressed in a book focusing on gendered trauma, given that gender seems incredibly relevant to this issue.

What is intimate partner violence though? It is an umbrella term that covers physical, sexual, emotional, psychological and verbal abusive behaviors, and stalking, in intimate partnerships. Intimate partner violence impacts millions of people in the United States and elsewhere. Globally statistics range from 10–69 percent of women being impacted and 40–70 percent of deaths by homicide among women being carried out by a husband, boyfriend or ex-partner of some kind (UN Women n.d.; WHO 2013). In the United States, one in five women and one in seven men have experienced intimate partner violence at some point in their life. The numbers for trans and nonbinary people are not really known but we do know that far too many trans feminine people of color globally and in the US are killed by current, past or potential partners. Even though intimate partner violence can happen to anyone in any kind of relationship, cis men seem to be responsible for the majority of the violence perpetrated in intimate relationships.

Of course, these numbers are not static and they shift depending on the multiple identities held by someone and the way in which power and oppression manifest in their lives. For example, Deaf and/or disabled boys and men are more likely to experience both childhood abuse, including sexual abuse, and intimate partner violence when compared to hearing and/or abled men. Trans, nonbinary and/or queer people, especially bisexual people, are also more likely to experience intimate partner violence than cis people and are often underserved by organizations that are historically more prepared to support cis women in very specific ways. The number of people impacted also increases when racialized identities and experiences are considered, with Latinx and Black people reporting higher levels of intimate partner violence, including a higher number of deaths by homicide for Latinx women.

Consequences

The consequences of intimate partner violence are far reaching. As well as the incredibly high number of deaths that this is responsible for, there are health issues that often arise from intimate partner violence. In the US, the CDC reports very binary statistics of 41 percent of women and 14 percent of men experiencing some form of physical injury as a result of intimate partner violence (CDC n.d.a). There are also other negative health outcomes that stem from intimate partner violence, such as chronic health conditions. When children are involved, we also know from the ACE (Adverse Childhood Events) study that their health is impacted when witnessing or experiencing domestic violence (CDC n.d.b). The CDC even calculates some of the financial cost of intimate partner violence, including lost work days, criminal proceedings and injury, estimating that, over the course of a lifetime, intimate partner violence will cost a woman around $103,000 and a man around $23,000 (CDC n.d.a).

From both the statistics, albeit very binary, and the cost, it is clear to see that intimate partner violence is much more impactful on women, especially women of color, and I would dare say, from the little we know, on trans and nonbinary people, especially if BIPOC and immigrant. We also know that statistically, although cis men also experience intimate partner violence, they are the main perpetrators of violence. When we consider the ubiquitous nature of toxic masculinity in dominant culture, and how toxic masculinity is also essential to the ongoing settler colonial project, this makes sense. Many studies of intimate partner violence, in fact, indicate that a recurring ingredient in these relational dynamics is control. If toxic masculinity is indeed about ownership and objectification of women/ femininity, then it makes sense that control becomes salient when considering intimate partner violence. Other factors that contribute to intimate partner violence include systemic poverty and alcohol and substance use. Given the higher levels of these issues in marginalized communities, it makes sense, once more, that the intersection of racism, cisgenderism, colonialism and ableism would lead to communities of color, as well as trans and immigrant communities being more impacted.

Secrecy and silence
This means that intimate partner violence cannot be addressed purely on an individual relationship level but rather it needs to be addressed on a systemic level, in schools, college campuses, criminal courts, hospitals, primary care clinics, family therapy,

faith communities, and in the media and so on. Instead, intimate partner violence is kept behind closed doors, where it tends to thrive, given that often physical violence is accompanied by controlling who the person is in contact with, isolating them from family, friends and communities, and making sure that they are economically, psychologically and emotionally dependent on their abusers.

Breaking the shroud of silence that surrounds intimate partner violence is incredibly challenging though. After all if women/feminine people's value, in dominant discourse, is dependent on being desired and even "owned" by a man through marriage or other familial bonds, then what does it say to the world if someone is being abused in their intimate partnerships? Many women/feminine people are either dependent or even feel responsible for the violence occurring in their relationships, and this can be nurtured by the people engaging in abusive behaviors in a number of ways. They might feel that if they were more caring, careful, docile or submissive these behaviors might stop. This pairs well with the ownership and control that those engaging in abusive behaviors might be trying to assert in their relationships, often as an expression of masculinity, when they might otherwise feel "out of control" feelings, such as being vulnerable or scared, which they do not know how to manage.

The issue of control through the policing of feminine bodies is particularly evident in the case of intimate partner violence leading to death amongst trans feminine people, especially women of color, and the legitimacy of the "trans panic defense," which is still upheld as valid in far too many courts. The trans panic defence involves claiming a level of "temporary insanity" where a person, usually a man, is so destabilized by finding out a partner is trans, usually trans feminine, that, in a moment of panic, he kills her. The trans panic defense is still viewed as valid in many courts but how is that possible? Westbrook and Schilt (2013) carry out an insightful analysis of how the sex/gender/sexuality system is maintained through societal determinations of gender, especially in relation to access to gendered spaces. They highlight that whereas cis people can maintain the same identity in all spaces, trans people will be determined to have different identities based on the interactions with specific spaces. For example, they might be identified based on their sex assigned at birth, their gender identity or the gender-related body modifications they might have pursued. The researchers highlight how policies to access public restrooms, league sports teams, shelters, prisons and other gendered integrated and segregated spaces are based on cisgenderist notions of "women" as vulnerable and "men" as dangerous, where often distinctions between men and women are conflated with specific genitals and bodies. These notions create "cultural anxiety on trans women" (Westbrook and Schilt 2013, p.20) as they are constructed to be, in the collective imagination, dangerous bodies that might "trick" cis heterosexual men into homosexual sex. This is the kind of argument used in the trans panic defense, which exploits cisgenderist, homophobic notions of trans feminine people, and trans feminine people of color in particular, as dangerous "others." Those dangerous "other" bodies might lead cis men away from heterosexuality through the subversion of the gender binary and the related "natural" (hetero)sexual system and, as such, they do not seem to deserve legal protection when harmed.

The issue of who needs protection from whom is central to the issue of intimate partner violence. Who are the bodies that are seen as worth protecting by the judicial system, as well as by police? The answer seems to lie in the chilling statistics already outlined. Feminine, disabled, trans, queer, Black, Brown, Indigenous, immigrant and sex workers' bodies seem to be the ones who are most disposable in dominant culture. It is enough to watch any major TV crime show to notice how different victims are depicted in very different ways depending on their gender, how they are racialized and so on. Unfortunately the bias is not limited to TV shows and it is evident in criminal and legal statistics. This is not necessarily something that judges or even police officers are doing "on purpose" but rather the bias is already built into every aspect of our lives. I remember being in court with my lawyer, my arm bandaged due to an injury, and the male judge asking me if I was trying to "make him feel sorry." I pointed out that this was what the doctor had done after I had been injured by my ex, who had been deemed as "not dangerous" enough to be removed from our apartment during a previous hearing. As the case was heard, the judge once more addressed me and asked me if I "really understood what I was doing" and the "damage" I would "inflict on this young graduate and the possible consequences to his career." I asked him if he had considered that I was a PhD student and whether he had considered the consequences on my career and life if I was not protected from my increasingly violent ex, especially given the statistics on death and intimate partner violence. The judge begrudgingly gave the order, under a new law in the UK, which enabled the police to arrest my ex without warning. The law had been recently changed due to the increased risk of violence, and even death, that giving a violent person warning that they would be arrested entailed. I don't believe that the judge was consciously thinking of gender or my body as less valuable than my ex, a cis white Anglo straight man. However, his actions and words implied a belief so deeply etched into our psyche that it can be challenging to view clearly as gendered bias. It is to the culture that makes intimate partner violence and other types of gendered violence so pervasive that we turn next.

4.4 Rape culture and sexual violence

Some people, starting mostly from 1970s second-wave feminists in what we currently know as the United States, would argue that we live in a rape culture; that is, a dominant culture that minimizes, condones and trivializes sexual assault and violence. The idea has encountered criticism and contributed to the rise of a movement pushing back on the ubiquitous and pervasive nature of sexual violence in intimate partnerships and beyond. Much as the conceptual framework can be debated, it would be challenging to deny that we live in a culture where most perpetrators of sexual violence are not prosecuted and even more often get away without consequences. People are often reluctant to report sexual assault whether it's perpetrated by an intimate partner or a stranger. Fear of repercussion, shame and ideas in dominant culture that somehow this could have been avoided if the victim had "behaved better/ been more aware/ dressed more appropriately" often drive survivors to not report what has happened to the authorities.

The practice of victim blaming is fairly pervasive in dominant culture and has contributed to the creation of the term "rape culture." Girls in particular are expected to behave within very narrow confines: on the one hand they are made fun of in movies and TV shows for being nerdy and often deemed unattractive, or coded as queer, if they do not conform to stereotypes of femininity. On the other hand they can be labelled as slutty if they do conform to these stereotypes, or even simply if a boy chooses to spread rumours or share stories of any potential sexual encounters with others. These tropes are played out in dominant culture again and again in movies such as *Mean Girls* or TV series like *13 Reasons Why*. Growing up I also remember relatives, especially women, commenting derogatorily about other women and even children and young people, labelling clothing, behaviors, make up, haircuts and language as "slutty" or not "lady-like" and often implying that these things would lead to potential assault or at the very least mistreatment by others because, after all, "what do they expect?" I have heard similar views again and again in the UK and the US so these are sadly not culturally unique. Whether we call it rape culture or not, I think we would be hard pressed to deny that we live in a dominant culture that depicts girls and women as morally responsible for the behaviors of boys and men, and as such as people to blame when these behaviors become "out of control" because after all "boys will be boys, right?"

#MeToo

In recent years, especially through social media platforms, we have also seen the rise of movements, led by women of color and especially Black and Indigenous women, that have stated that enough is enough. One of those movements has become known as the "#MeToo" movement. Initially this was started by Tarana Burke, an African-American woman and youth worker, ten years prior to the tweet by Alyssa Milano in October 2017 using the same #MeToo hashtag. Tarana was moved by listening again and again to stories of sexual violence by young girls of color and decided to break the silence in which abuse and violence thrive. Ten years later a group of famous cis white women, starting with Alyssa Milano's tweet, would make this movement visible through their celebrity status, and millions of people, especially women, reported online stories of sexual assault, abuse, domestic violence and rape. Once more we can see how the intersection of race and gender led to the movement to become visible in dominant culture only when white bodies were in the spotlight, rather than Black, Brown, Indigenous, trans, queer, nonbinary, immigrant bodies.

In *Life Isn't Binary* (2019), my co-author Meg-John Barker and I, write how the #MeToo movement was also more complex than a simple binary of victims rising against perpetrators. While many women and survivors of all genders felt they could finally speak out and be a part of something greater than themselves, other survivors of sexual violence found the hashtag to be triggering. All of the sudden social media feeds did indeed show how widespread misogynistic sexual violence truly is. This was challenging for many survivors and empowering for others. Some survivors were ready to—and wanted to—share their stories out loud. Other survivors were muting their feed so they could still be on social media, as this might be a source of social support, but not feel constantly triggered. To trouble the issue further, male and nonbinary survivors felt uncertain about using the hashtag, and some were even berated for doing so because this was not "their movement," even though they had also been subject to the same sexual violence rooted in patriarchy. As we ask in our book: who was inside or outside of the movement? Who did the movement belong to?

Many Black women also felt alienated since they knew the hashtag had been started by a Black woman, but now white celebrities were garnering all the attention. Some felt that the increased attention was due to the fact that sexual violence against white women is seen as unacceptable whereas violence against Black women is seen as the norm. Suddenly some Black women who had been at the beginning of the movement, felt the movement had been co-opted and appropriated by white women, who also participated in perpetrating systemic violence against them. All the people involved in this messy situation were survivors of sexual violence. Many were also subject to systemic racial violence, while others were not. The racial violence was also inextricably linked with the sexual violence many had experienced, because their bodies were sexualized in certain ways due to being racialized in certain ways. All of this violence was, and is, also gendered, as we discussed earlier.

And in the midst of this trauma, visibility and resistance, there was/is the desire to be seen, to not be erased, to not be pushed out of the movement, the desire to heal together. Given that most trauma happens in the context of relationships, it is in the context of relationships that we might find the potential for healing. However, relationships are messy and complicated. They do not happen in a vacuum, they happen in larger and smaller systems, as discussed in this book. The #MeToo movement was born, among other things, from a desire to connect and to find the intimacy of shared experience with other survivors.

It was also born, though, out of the reality of violence against girls and women of color, especially Black women. And this violence has deeper roots, as discussed in this book. For example, studies in the UK and the US have shown that children, even at a very young age, have a strong pro-white and anti-Black bias unless they are intentionally exposed to Black history and role models. It seems clear that the combination of cisgenderism and racism, including implicit bias, would create a dominant culture in which feminine Black, Brown and Indigenous bodies are viewed as less valuable.

This ripples through all aspects of our lives, including the ways in which we were parented and parent our children. For example, it is a well-known fact, in the US, that Black parents or any parents of Black children need to give "the talk" about the police and how to interact with them to their children at a fairly young age. This is because they are more likely to encounter systemic violence at the hands of police officers, even when very young. White parents, by and large, do not need to do this. Indigenous parents need to talk to their children, especially girls and gender expansive children, about the risk of being abducted and/or groomed for trafficking and sexual exploitation. Parents of disabled and Deaf children would be wise to talk with their children about the risk of sexual abuse but sadly rarely do as they too, unless disabled themselves, might infantilize their children and underestimate the risks they encounter in an ableist world.

Childhood, ownership and consent

As discussed earlier when addressing purity balls, parenting is another arena in which aspects of dominant culture, including rape culture, become evident. We often learn at a very young age what it means to be a boy or a girl, and rarely do we learn that there are also options to not be bound by our sex assigned at birth in many ways. This is when the seeds of toxic cisgenderism, racism and so on can be planted, if we are not vigilant as adult caregivers and, even then, we might still find ourselves swimming upstream against the current of dominant culture. For example, often parents treat and talk about their children as property or perpetuate power dynamics that set them up for potential abuse. This is often not done intentionally. Innocuous phrases such as "be good for grandpa" or "do what dad tells you" or the ever pervasive "because I say so" set children up as less agentic than adults.

This coupled with the lack of consent children often experience when it comes to touch, such as being pushed to hug and kiss relatives whether they want to or not, can lead to children not understanding that they have the power to say no, that they don't have to be "good" for adults or do what adults say, and that they do not need to be silent if someone is interacting with them inappropriately.

Parents and caregivers, however, are not the only culprits in this area. Schools also have a lot to answer for. Many educational environments, for example, reward compliance and repress challenges to authority, regardless of whether children and young people have cause to challenge said authorities or not. This is very evident in the physical, sexual, emotional and psychological abuse perpetrated against disabled, Deaf, trans, nonbinary and queer children and youth by adults in school environments. Studies indicate again and again, for example, that young people with these marginalized identities are harassed, sexualized and abused not just by peers but far too often by adults. Once more the combination of certain identities seems to be conducive to certain bodies not being viewed as worthy of protection as others. Often Deaf and disabled boys, for example, experience much higher rates of abuse than their hearing and abled counterparts because their Deafness or disability not only makes them vulnerable to abuse but also emasculates them to some degree, within the dominant paradigm.

Trans, nonbinary and/or queer children and youth are also viewed differently than their cisgender, heterosexual counterparts within this framework. Somehow their gender identities and expressions and/or their sexuality seem to set them apart for being treated as hypersexual, and as such much more prone to harassment and abuse by both peers and adults. Adults might also collude by not protecting these children even when they do not perpetrate the abuse themselves. For example, some educators express victim-blaming views that imply that trans, nonbinary and/or queer children and youth are bringing the abuse upon themselves by displaying traits outside normative confines. All the statistics about harassment and abuse, sadly and unsurprisingly, increase at the intersection of these named identities and racialized identities and experiences. This means that usually BIPOC disabled, Deaf, trans, nonbinary and queer children and youth experience higher levels of systemic violence within the education system.

If we take a moment to go back to the beginning, the policing of children and young people's bodies through violence makes sense within the ongoing settler colonial project. Bodies that do not fit into cishetero, white, settler colonial narratives are troubling from the beginning and, as such, subject to closer scrutiny and control from every system. It is those systems that I address in the next chapter, before moving on to the final chapter where I attempt to offer some practices to heal our relationship with gender. Before moving on to how a rigid gender binary is manifested systemically in dominant culture, let's take a moment to practice an educational stretch.

Educational stretch: the impact of systemic violence in our relationships

First, take a moment to notice how you are doing. I am addressing a lot of trauma that might impact your body in specific ways. I know that I found this book challenging to write and I had to take frequent breaks while writing. Please do not push yourself beyond your window of tolerance! It's ok to take care of ourselves, even though we might live in a dominant culture where it's not always ok or possible to do so. If and when you're ready, go back to the gender map you created in Chapter 3.

Take a moment to consider how your assumptions about gender, the expectations you and/or your communities hold, and the blame and/or shame that might be held in your body are impacted by the topics addressed in this chapter. For example, how does cisgenderism manifest in your life, your family, relationships, friendships, in your work, faith community, hobbies and so on? Do you notice toxic masculinity around you? What does this look like in your own life, in your relationships, work and communities? Again, take some deep breaths; no matter how much work we do, none of us are immune to dominant culture. It's the air we breathe, and particles get in, whether we like it or not, so try to hold yourself in as much self-compassion as you can muster right now.

Finally, if you have the capacity, I invite you to consider how violence might show up in your life, your relationships, your work and your communities. Do some of the issues raised in this chapter resonate with your experience? If so, in what way? Are your experiences different or have they not been addressed in this chapter? If so, what difference does that make? For example, you might feel turned off, erased or excluded. These can be challenging thoughts and emotions to sit with. Take a moment to record your thoughts, feelings and reactions to this educational stretch. Then take a little break to take care of you and please be kind and gentle with yourself, if you are able.

Summary

- Objectification theory offers a framework to understand how girls and women are often acculturated to view themselves as objects offered to, and evaluated through, the male gaze and its values.

- Objectification of girls and women also impacts boys and men and dehumanizes their sexuality. In this framework, men/masculine people are not viewed as autonomous agents but rather as out of control and driven by their sexual needs above all others.

- We cannot view gender as separate from other aspects of our identities and experiences. This means that queer relationships and sexualities are also impacted by dominant ideas of gender.

- The combination of objectification and the dominant idea that sexuality is only the domain of young and middle adulthood means that usually disabled people are infantilized within the overculture. Disabled people are often viewed as vulnerable, and therefore potential sexual victims, or as having "perverse/deviant" sexualities.

- Racialized identities and dynamics are also essential to consider when discussing dominant ideas of gender in relationships. Dominant discourses of gender are also white dominant discourses. This means that bodies are not only racialized in dominant discourses but also sexualized and gendered upon the foundations of settler colonialism and white supremacy.

- Objectification is also interwoven with the idea of ownership. If women and femininity exist for and are dependent on the male gaze, the latter is then inherently superior and agentic. The agency of the male gaze is then often expressed through the implication of ownership.

- Parents are usually encouraged in dominant culture to view children as an extension of themselves, including their own gendered expectations.

- Toxic masculinity is not inherent to being a man/masculine person but rather it indicates a set of norms contributing to a cultural mindset that perpetuates harmful stereotypes and rigid gender binaries.

- Toxic masculinity is not automatically and only upheld by men. While men are encouraged to adhere to toxic masculine ideals in dominant culture, all of us are invited into the dance of toxic masculinity through societal scripts.

- Toxic cisgenderism is not inherent to cis people but rather it's a "prejudicial ideology" that assumes cisgender identities and experiences as inherently natural, desirable, and as such superior to, any other gender identities and experiences.

- Cisgenderism also interacts with all other aspects of our identities and expressions. For example, it is far safer for white people to express their gender in more expansive ways, whereas Black, Brown and Indigenous bodies are more closely scrutinized, policed and punished for transgressing gender norms.

- Ableism also intersects with cisgenderism, as any deviation from cisgenderism can be viewed as a response to being disabled rather than as an authentic identity and/or expression.

- Intimate partner violence is an umbrella term that covers

physical, sexual, emotional, psychological and verbal abusive behaviors, and stalking, in intimate partnerships.

- Intimate partner violence is very common and is responsible for nearly half the number of women killed by homicide in the United States. Furthermore, despite being described as a public health concern by agencies such as the CDC (Center for Disease Control) in the US, many educators and therapists do not receive enough training on how to address intimate partner violence, and especially teen dating violence, which is also common.

- The number of people impacted by intimate partner violence is increased when racialized identities and experiences are considered, with Latinx and Black people reporting higher levels of intimate partner violence, including a higher number of deaths by homicide for Latinx women.

- Intimate partner violence cannot be addressed purely on an individual relationship level but rather it needs to be addressed on a systemic level, in schools, college campuses, criminal courts, hospitals, primary care clinics, family therapy, faith communities, in the media and so on.

- The issue of who needs protection from whom is central to the issue of intimate partner violence. Who are the bodies that are seen as worth protecting by the judicial system, as well as by police? The answer seems to lie in the chilling statistics already outlined. Feminine, disabled, trans, queer, Black, Brown, Indigenous, immigrant and sex workers' bodies seem to be the ones who are most disposable in dominant culture.

- Rape culture can be defined as a dominant culture that minimizes, condones and trivializes sexual assault and violence. The idea has encountered both criticism and contributed to the rise of a movement pushing back on the ubiquitous and pervasive nature of sexual violence in intimate partnerships and beyond.
- The #MeToo movement was born, among other things, from a desire to connect and to find the intimacy of shared experience with other survivors. It was also born, though, out of the reality of violence against girls and women of color, especially Black women.
- The combination of cisgenderism and racism, including implicit bias, creates a dominant culture in which feminine Black, Brown and Indigenous bodies are viewed as less valuable.
- Often BIPOC disabled, Deaf, trans, nonbinary and queer children and youth experience higher levels of systemic violence within their families, communities and the education system.

CHAPTER 5

Systems

In the previous chapter I explored how ideas of gender in dominant culture influence relationships, especially, but not exclusively, romantic and sexual relationships. I highlighted how objectification impacts a range of people and how it connects with the idea of ownership. The latter manifests not just in intimate relationships but also in parenting, especially the parenting of girls by men. I addressed the concepts of toxic masculinity and cisgenderism, the reality of intimate partner violence, and the larger context of sexual violence and rape culture.

In this chapter, I turn to larger systemic issues. How is a rigid gender binary not only condoned and endorsed, but also reproduced, within dominant culture? I address how seven structural components of our everyday lives reproduce traumatic gendered dynamics.

I start from the legal system, given that this seems an organic segue from discussing sexual violence and rape culture. I then go on to address politics, the judicial and criminal systems, architecture and the design of public spaces. After this I consider the medical system, the education system, and finally the field of mental health, in which I spend much of my working time as a systemic psychotherapist.

What I can cover in a single chapter is fairly limited compared to the vastness of topics such as law and gender. There are many more books and papers on each of these areas which you may want to follow up. What I provide here is but an overview to illustrate how a rigid gender binary seeps into all of our major societal structures.

5.1 Law

I mentioned briefly, in the previous chapter, how laws can increase or decrease risk for people who seek to leave relationships in which there is intimate partner violence. Given that legal structures are part of a country's governance, it makes sense that the law would be shaped by—and be a part of—oppressive forces such as ongoing settler colonialism, racism, patriarchy, ableism, classism, misogyny and so on.

Legal scholar Kimberlé Williams Crenshaw, for example, addressed the specific interaction of racism and misogyny and how this plays a particular role in the life of Black girls and women when they interact with legal, criminal and judicial systems (Crenshaw 1989). This interaction is what her theory of intersectionality was built on. These critiques of existing legal structures are focused on power structures, and a binary conceptualization of gender is part of these. So, when we consider gender in a legal context, how does the law contribute to reproducing dominant discourses of gender?

One of the most basic ways in which this happens is who gets to legally define terms such as sex and gender. This is essential as laws on sex and/or gender discrimination—depending on the country and chosen wording—might or might not protect trans people. For example, in the US, under several administrations, for nearly two decades, there seemed to be a legal consensus that federal sex discrimination laws could be applied to protect trans people. However, more recently this has been put into question by a few decisions where trans status was not considered to be a protected category under existing federal legislation.

In the UK, the Gender Recognition Act (GRA) was passed in 2004 and came into effect in 2005, as a specific piece of legislation that enabled trans people to have their gender identity recognized but that still enabled discrimination to occur against trans people in certain settings. In 2017, the Scottish government published a review denouncing some of the GRA practices as intrusive and placing an undue burden on trans people. The GRA also interacts with the Equality Act (2010) so that a trans woman recognized as such through the GRA would have her status as a woman protected under the Equality Act but one not recognized through the GRA would not. These legal definitions and procedures around sex and gender, therefore, matter an awful lot, especially, but not exclusively, for trans people.

Debates about who counts as what legally can be placed within a larger historical framework. For example, it has now been well documented that the suffragette movement, campaigning for women's rights to vote, had a racism problem, both in the US and UK, although it manifested differently in those countries. In the US, it quickly became evident that, while white women were trying to be equal to their father, brothers and husbands, Black women were fighting both for themselves and Black men to have the right to vote. Suffrage for them was not just a matter of gender but also of racial equality. Black abolitionists such as Frederick Douglas were supportive of women's rights but the same could not be said for many suffragettes, who only supported (white) women's right to vote and were not necessarily supportive of abolition or equality for Black people. In fact, even those white women who were supportive of the abolition of slavery were often quick to abandon this issue if they felt it would hurt their cause for (white) women's right to vote.

In the UK that problem might not have been as stark but leading figures such as Emmeline Pankhurst upheld colonialism. In fact, some of the UK white suffragettes were "appalled" that Maori women in one of their colonies could vote whereas they couldn't (Jones 2015). We can understand then that many of the historical legal issues about who can vote, own property, or be recognized as having a certain nationality or belonging to a tribal nation, are not just linked to gender but also to how we are racialized.

In more recent times, the UK government, under the Labor party and while still in the European Union, changed immigration laws in 2000. Under the new 2000 rule, for example, a child born in the UK to a parent with citizenship in another European country and one with UK citizenship could get UK citizenship automatically only if the parents were married or if the UK parent was deemed to be the "mother." I found this out when my child was born. At that point I had lived in the UK as an EU citizen for ten years. My child's father was a UK citizen, and named on the birth certificate, but our child, at that point in time, had no right to automatic British citizenship. We could either petition for naturalization as a British citizen, leave things as they were or get married. My gender literally dictated my child's citizenship. The argument was that if I were the mother *and* a UK citizen then my child's Britishness could not be denied, whereas the father could always be disputed. This, of course, did not explain why marriage solved anything. After all, I could have been married to a UK citizen and had the child with someone else, potentially, as I pointed out to the immigration official.

This seemed to be more an issue of ethnic purity compounded by gender, enabled by a law reform that sought to decrease the number of children born to EU parents who could claim UK citizenship. Around the same time we also discovered that in Italy our child had to take on the surname of their father if we were legally married, something that has recently been challenged successfully in court by an Italian-Brazilian couple. In both countries, we found ourselves dealing with laws around gender and marriage that had nothing to do with how our child should be legally recognized, in an ideal world, but everything to do with upholding patriarchal and xenophobic values.

One of the most heinous examples of how the legal system perpetuates violence and oppression based on gender is the legal sterilization of disabled girls and women. Even though, officially, eugenics is no longer endorsed by most scientists and governments, in practice disabled girls and women, especially those with learning disabilities, are being sterilized against their will every day. This is a practice often upheld by their own parents either when the girls are still minors or in cases where parents gain guardianship. This practice continues to be justified not only by caregivers and families but also by governments, despite the fact that disability justice advocates have been vocal against these practices for decades. In fact, the *Convention on the Rights of Persons with Disabilities* directly addresses this issue and the Committee on the Rights of the Child has clearly named the forced sterilization of disabled girls as a form of violence.

The International Federation of Gynecology and Obstetrics (FIGO) issued in June 2011 some new guidelines on contraceptive sterilization and informed consent that preclude guardians and/or family members from consenting to the sterilization of disabled girls and women without their own consent. Those guidelines also stated the right of disabled girls and women and their representative organizations and networks to be included in the development of legislation that impacts their sexual and reproductive rights (see IFHHRO 2011). Sadly guidelines are just that and it takes political will for oppressive legislations to change, which is why this is the area I turn to next.

5.2 Politics

The issue of gender in politics, like gender and law, is a well-discussed one by much more knowledgeable and authoritative experts in those fields. For the purpose of the present book, I'd like to touch on a few major issues that illustrate how certain power structures continue to be upheld regardless of whether we live in a democratic regime or not. The most obvious issue seems to be that of representation. Very few politicians on a global level fall outside of the gender binary in any way, so much so that any trans and/or nonbinary politician who is elected usually makes the news. In fact even if we stay strictly within a binary view of gender, there is a clear imbalance in politics, with cis men dominating the field on a global scale.

In 2017 the percentage of (supposedly cis) women holding parliamentary positions on a global scale was 23.4 percent. This was just a 0.1 percent increase from the previous report, despite increased participation by women in politics (Inter-Parliamentary Union 2018). However, representation is not purely a numbers game. Research has shown that women are more likely to advocate for issues such as gender-related violence, education and women's economic independence (Inter-Parliamentary Union 2018). As one of my friends and amazing council women for

Minneapolis, Andrea Jenkins, once stated in a keynote, being in the room changes the room. Who is in those parliamentary rooms changes the topics that are considered and discussed.

Sadly even women often only focus on gender as a purely binary issue. There have been recent changes and we've seen not only trans and/or nonbinary elected officials but also cis candidates discussing the needs of transgender Americans in the latest presidential debates in the US in 2019. I believe this only happened because of having trans White House staffers under the previous administration and an increasing number of trans and/or nonbinary local political representatives.

This is why the homogeneity of politicians in most countries globally is something to pay attention to and that needs changing. Homogeneity in this context is not just about gender but also race, Indigeneity, disability, religion and so much more. If our gendered experiences cannot be neatly separated from other aspects of our identities and experiences, then surely homogeneity of our representatives is not desirable. It is unsurprising that in countries like the UK then, there is not just a homogeneity of identities and experiences but also of views. This makes change in any direction slow and difficult, if possible. How can challenging rigid gender binaries in this context help? One of the issues of homogeneity is that not only do politicians tend to the same discourses over and over again, but also that the interests they're focusing on are those of people similar to them.

Challenging rigid gender binaries might help loosen these political borders. If we can no longer assume a rigid and impenetrable frontier between the categories of "men" and "women," then what could be possible for all of us, not just us trans and/or nonbinary people? As long as homogeneity rules, the political arena is narrow and benefits an incredibly small number of people. Anything that challenges this homogeneity has the potential to broaden political discourse and lead to greater benefit for a larger number of people.

This, of course, requires a leadership shift on a global level, something that it's incredibly challenging to achieve, as we can see from that 0.1 percent increase in women in global parliamentary seats. Political leadership shifts are challenging given that most people who are not generally cis men (and in many countries such as the US and UK cis white men) simply do not have the social, political and intergenerational capital to become politicians. The ongoing settler colonial project and the patriarchy go hand in hand in so many ways; political representation is just one of them. As well as intergenerational trauma, discussed in earlier chapters, people also have access to intergenerational, historical, social and cultural power. This is what perpetuates the homogeneity of politicians. A leadership shift in politics on both local and global levels requires a disruption of this accumulation of intergenerational, historical, social and cultural power. Let's take a moment to reflect on why this might require not just an external shift but also an internal re-orientation when it comes to leadership in politics.

Thoughtful moment: what we learn about leadership and gender from politics

You've been invited, throughout this book, to reflect on what you have learned about gender from history, your family, your own experience and the relationships around you. Now I would like to invite you to think about what you have learned about gender and leadership from politics. Politics does not mean just who is representing you in your country's Parliament or in City Council but also who is viewed as a leader.

Take a moment to think about examples of leaders through-out your life. This could be presidents of a country, monarchs, political representatives, but also principals, clinic directors, chair of organizational boards and so on. First of all, who comes to mind when you think about leaders and, more specifically, political leaders? Do they look a particular way? What do you imagine their gender, race, ethnicity, class, religion, disability status, citizenship and education level to be? Are there specific people who come to mind? You can take some notes if you like to illustrate the landscape of political leadership in your mind. When you look at this landscape, is this in line with your own values? Is this landscape in line with your own identities and experiences? If so, in what way? If not, why not? Is there anything surprising when you look at this landscape?

Now take a few more moments to reflect on what qualities come to mind when you think about political leaders. You might even want to jot them down or draw them. When you look at those qualities through the lens of gender, what happens? Are they gendered qualities or not? Are they gendered even despite your own beliefs? We're constantly absorbing stories from the world around us. What are the stories about gender, leadership and politics that you have absorbed from the environment around you so far? If you want, you can write your reflections down or record them in a voice memo.

5.3 Judicial and criminal systems

Law and politics are two of the major arenas where decisions are made, including the decision of what are the matters worthy of legislative action. The judicial and criminal systems are the channels through which those laws and political decisions are enforced. I mentioned earlier legal scholar Kimberlé Crenshaw and her work on the intersection of race and gender (1989). Her early work was very much focused on how the experiences of Black girls and women in the judicial and criminal systems are inherently different to those of Black boys and men as well as to those of white girls and women. It's at the intersection of race and gender that a specific type of policing and punishment occurs, and this is a place she shines a light on with her work.

Crenshaw points out that, when it comes to the judicial and criminal systems, women have pushed for the recognition of systemic issues such as intimate partner violence, moving those from the realm of the person to the political. However identity politics, as she argues, can be limiting if it erases and/or conflates the differences between us, such as race. We cannot look at race and gender as separate categories if we want to understand the experiences of Black girls and women in those contexts.

I want to start from Crenshaw's theory of intersectionality because I believe it to be key in helping us understand how discriminatory the judicial and criminal systems are. In a way those systems are the executive branches of the ongoing settler colonial project in countries like the US. It's not surprising then that the ways in which they police communities and bodies closely resemble a colonial, racist, patriarchal, ableist agenda. This is exactly what these systems were created to do. If this seems a bold statement, I invite you to review some of the further reading resources for this chapter.

What I mean by my bold statement—and what many researchers more expert in those fields than I have discussed—is that people are criminalized and imprisoned in ways that continue to penalize Black, Brown, Indigenous, disabled, trans, queer, immigrant, and sex workers' bodies in many countries. Those bodies continue to be profitable commodities in the neo-liberal prison industrial complex of certain countries and serve capitalism in specific ways. Given that most prisons and immigration detention centers are privately owned, and that prison inmates are usually paid cents per hour for their labor in the US, those bodies are commodities that serve the interest of larger corporations who profit from their labor. This seems to bring up the question of who is protected by judicial courts and the police, and who is being policed in discriminatory ways and then introduced into the school-to-prison pipeline that several authors have discussed, at least in a US context. So, what does gender have to do with all of this?

As Crenshaw and many others have argued, gender cannot be separated from other ways in which our bodies are legislated, judged and policed. However, gender also impacts these systems in specific ways. For example, there is plenty of research, from the 1970s onwards, indicating how women are treated during judicial trials related to sexual assault because of their gender. Issues such as what they were wearing, whether they had been drinking and their sexual histories are suddenly on trial, rather than the person who has assaulted them in the first place. This is something that surfaces in many countries at various times and is still an issue now. In many ways, the issue is about women's credibility in court and whether they are reliable and honest witnesses. This is an issue that is deeply enmeshed with constructions of femininity as circuitous, manipulative, vengeful and untrustworthy.

Other constructions of femininity that hurt women in courtrooms and in the penal system are those of femininity as "naturally" caring and maternal. This means that, most of the time, women are given much harsher sentences for crimes that are considered violent and, especially for those that seem to go against their "maternal nature," such as infanticide. The exception to this is the murder of disabled children, which is still not punished as harshly by judicial courts as the murder of abled children by their parents. In those cases ableism seems to trump sexism and women who kill their disabled children are not viewed as heartless murderers but rather as exhausted victims (see Bottoms *et al.* 2011).

When we look more closely then, even though there are differences that are based on gender, the discourse becomes murkier depending on what other variables are in the mix. For example, in the US, when various intersections are considered, it's often young Black men with lower levels of income and education who seem to be at the highest risk of being incarcerated. They are often more likely to be kept in prison longer as their sentences are adjusted up rather than down (Holzer, Offner and Sorensen 2005; Pettit and Western 2004).

Many of the differences that we see emerge again and again in the literature on judicial and criminal systems seem to pivot around the idea of who is "worthy of protection" and who is viewed as "redeemable" versus inherently delinquent. It's in this melting pot of anti-Blackness, racism, xenophobia, sexism, transphobia, ableism, classism, Islamophobia and colonialism that judicial and criminal systems operate. These systems are not inherently unbiased, yet they're often portrayed as the ultimate arbiters of justice that, while portrayed as egalitarian, more often than not reproduce the same disparities that shape other systems.

It's probably not surprising that often the people delivering those systems are not the people most impacted by these symptoms. For example, in the US, most of the judges and court officials are not young, Black men from lower income backgrounds, even though the latter are severely impacted by these systems. Similarly to politics, a change in leadership and representation would probably impact outcome. However, many racial and gender justice activists are not just calling for a change of leadership in these arenas, but rather questioning the legitimacy of those systems by calling for prison abolition and the re-imagining of a world without police. Those subjects deserve, and have, their own research, so it's with an invitation to explore those possibilities further that I want to end this section and move on to consider how even public space is shaped by a rigid gender binary.

5.4 Architecture and the design of public spaces

The judicial and criminal systems are not the only ways to control and police who belongs where. Architecture can also have this function. How spaces are conceived, designed, implemented and organized also tells the story of dominant discourse. A hopefully obvious example is that of how diaper changing stations were only recently added to "men's bathrooms." This change seems to have slowly followed changing discourse about the division of labor when it comes to child-rearing. It's also a change that we see in some places and not others. In fact, let's back it up a moment and consider the division of bathrooms into a rigid binary of men and women.

In many places, men's and women's bathrooms are the only two options, with occasionally a third option generally designated as an accessible bathroom and/or family restroom, or, very rarely, as an all genders restroom. This is where the rigid colonial construction of gender as a binary is enshrined in the architecture of public spaces. Where I live, one of the local hospitals managed to build recently an entire six-floor building for specialist care with hundreds of offices but only two public all genders restroom on the sixth floor. It's obvious that nonbinary people, disabled people with carers of a gender different than their own, or parents and caregivers of children of a gender different than their own, are not at the forefront of architectural design. If we were, there would be many more bathrooms accessible to all! Those bathrooms would, of course, also serve people who might not fit into stereotypical gender expressions, such as masculine-looking women and femme-looking men and would likely reduce the risk of harassment and violence for all.

This is, therefore, not just about bathrooms, but rather about who is considered worthy of being given access to public spaces and facilities. For example, a child with long hair was told that some trouble was to be "expected" if they used the boys' bathroom in school, even though there really wasn't a viable alternative. The message was clear: if you don't conform, the space cannot welcome you and we cannot protect you. We receive these types of messages every day through space. For example, not many work spaces have lactation rooms, making it clear that people who are breastfeeding are not necessarily expected to be part of the workforce. Other spaces might have ramps for patients or concert goers but not doctors or performers, again making it clear who belongs where in dominant culture. Spaces tell us stories all the time: stories we internalize and often start to believe.

Architecture is, of course, not just about structures but also lighting, colors, signage and so on. Public buildings often also include historical representations through pictures or murals.

Who is represented there? Which genders, races, ethnicities, tribal nations, disabilities? How are they represented? Have you ever seen yourself represented in pictures, murals or statues? If so, did you take this for granted or was it novel? Take a moment to notice, next time you navigate a public space, what and who you see. What are the colors around you in which spaces? Do they tell a story about gender or any other aspects of identity and experience? Architecture is another system too often dominated by cis white men and, just like other systems, this too has been shaken up by activists in the field who feel that designing more inclusive and equitable spaces has the potential to change our behaviors and the ways in which we interact with space.

In 2018, in the US, a project called "Stalled!" won the AIA (American Institute for Architects) Innovation Award. This project was a response to the various legal battles that more conservatives politicians were raising to overturn the previous administration's decision that Title IX protected transgender people when using a bathroom aligning with their gender identity. This project was brought together by historian Susan Stryker, architect Joel Sanders and legal scholar Terry Kogan. Bathrooms of course have often been part of movements for civil rights for Black people, women and disabled people, as well as for transgender and/or nonbinary people. After all, if we cannot have access to a space that allows us to fulfil one of the most basic bodily functions, how can we have a place in public life? It's therefore not surprising that bathrooms are often both a symbol and a utilitarian struggle within social justice movements.

Architectural design, in fact, is often driven by inherent bias where the user is imagined to be cisgender, not disabled, and male. This is not surprising given both the male dominance in the field and the fact that most of the people commissioning architectural work are also men. Once again, systems and structures reproduce themselves, in the case of architecture, literally and materially. We see in the design of space, especially public space, the ongoing colonial dominance of both land and people, unless this is intentionally questioned.

Green spaces, for example, are separated from living, work and public offices and confined to specific areas. Those spaces are often near-absent in certain neighborhoods, once more reproducing the same inequalities we see again and again in our societies. In a way the organization and design of spaces is a vivid representation of the separation between land and people, perpetuating the idea of land ownership and the policing of bodies through structures that are often only accessible and/or welcoming to specific bodies.

5.5 Medicine

I have mentioned how, in architecture, the baseline user is often imagined to be cisgender, not disabled, and male. If we add white to the mix, we also have the imagined baseline patient in medicine. The medical-industrial complex is another system shaped by the disparities inherent to the ongoing settler colonial project. The fact that the baseline is clearly the cisgender white male is evident in issues such as the lower level of knowledge, and/or public health investment, when it comes to reproductive and sexual health issues, transgender health issues, and cardiac issues in women, especially Black women. Researchers often argue that before they can look at "minority populations" they need to have a clear sense of the baseline population. What is inherent in that statement is that, in many Anglo countries, what they mean by baseline population is white, cisgender, not disabled, younger and usually divided according to a rigid gender binary of male/female. Everyone else is not viewed as being part of the baseline population but rather as a minority and specialist interest.

This is significant because measurements, assessment tools and interventions are then designed for this "baseline population," and medical providers are also trained within this paradigm. This means that often providers are hardly prepared to be in the room with actual patients who don't fall within the parameters they were trained within. The issue of cardiac issues in Black women in the US is a telling example of this. One in two Black women in the US has some form of heart disease and they're also twice as likely to have a stroke compared to white women (Rosenberg *et al.* 1999). Yet, if you picture who is most likely to have a heart attack, or a stroke, chances are that you might have imagined a white man in that situation. Sadly the same goes for medical providers who are less likely to notice symptoms of heart attacks and strokes in people who don't fall within stereotypical, albeit medically inaccurate, parameters.

There is copious literature on the subject of bias in medicine, from bias within the profession—that is who is most likely to be viewed as a competent provider (unsurprisingly cis white men make an appearance here)—to patients being treated in discriminatory ways because of their gender, race, ethnicity, disabled status, age, religion and so on (see the further reading for Chapter 5 at the end of the book). Despite the research that keeps indicating bias, few, if any, interventions have been successful in eradicating such bias. By and large medical schools tend to be led by older, cis white men and, given that systems usually stay the same unless really challenged to change it is no surprise that those medical systems reproduce themselves over time, research findings notwithstanding. Just as with all other systems discussed so far, this is not just about leadership but also about how the systems work, who they work for and who is failed by and within them.

Disparities around gender and race clearly indicate who the medical system is failing: women, transgender people, queer people, Black people, Indigenous people, disabled people and people from lower income and educational backgrounds. This list might begin to seem familiar. The medical-industrial complex is yet another system that fails people it was never meant to serve. By doing so, medicine reproduces the ongoing settler colonial, misogynistic, ableist and transphobic violence that, by now, you might feel well acquainted with. It seems unnecessary to list all the disparities in the medical field. Unsurprisingly, the people most impacted are those who are still viewed as the most disposable by dominant culture. This is something that we have come back to again and again throughout the book and that sadly we will keep coming back to throughout this chapter.

One aspect I would like to touch on before moving on to education is that of the sick/healthy binary, given that this is, in itself, often gendered according to the rigid colonial binary I keep examining here. The very notion of femininity seems to carry within itself a connotation of sickness. For example, in dominant Anglo discourses women tend to be viewed as less rational, more emotional and therefore inherently more prone to hysteria. Even though nobody, hopefully, is likely to be accused of hysteria by a medical professional in 2019, far too often women are viewed by providers as exaggerating their symptoms and their reliability in issues such as reporting pain levels is questioned. Research indicates how women are treated differently to men when it comes to pain reporting, treatment and management, for example (Hamburg *et al.* 2002; Heston and Lewis 1992; Samulowitz *et al.* 2018).

Gender also seems pivotal in the discrimination experienced by transgender and/or nonbinary people who, again and again, report attention being paid to irrelevant issues such as their genitals and trans status—even when they go into the doctor to address things like colds or broken limbs. There seems, therefore, to be an inherent quality of hegemonic cisgenderist masculinity in the construction of health and healthy, as it pertains to the current state of medicine. This is unsurprising given the pervasive andronormativity already discussed in the field. Therefore, it could be argued, everyone who strays away from this norm could be viewed as inherently "sick" in some way, just by virtue of not being a cis, white, not disabled man.

At the same time, given the pervasive andronormativity and gender bias in medicine, it's paradoxically challenging for people who are not cis, white, not disabled men to be taken seriously as patients. Caught in the paradox of "inherently sick" and therefore not worthy to be considered "truly ill," many of us fall through the cracks of the medical-industrial complex by being viewed as unreliable witnesses, unworthy of care or by simply being erased. If this seems another bold statement, I invite you to consider the disparities in medical treatment and outcome mentioned earlier in this chapter.

5.6 Education

Much of what we have discussed so far could be viewed as stemming from the educational system. After all education is where we are supposed to learn how to be in the world and how to participate in all the systems already mentioned here so far.

What is the role of education, though, within ongoing settler colonial states? The US, Canada and Australia all have sadly illuminating histories when it comes to the education system and the process of settler colonialism. In all these countries, taking children away from their families and tribes to be placed in residential schools where they would be punished for using their language or adhering to their customs was pretty common practice at the beginning of their existence as sovereign states. In those cases the role of education was to disconnect these children from place, family and community, and to eradicate their language and culture so that those could be replaced by the language and culture of the colonizers. Over the past decade, we have witnessed an increasing disclosure of the horrors perpetrated in the name of education in those schools. Just recently, in Canada, the names of 2800 Indigenous children who died in residential schools were included in a new National Residential School Student Death Register. This registry is still about 1600 names short according to the National Centre for Truth and Reconciliation, bringing that number up to 4000 dead children, out of the 150,000+ Indigenous children removed by force from their families by the state.

Education can, therefore, never be neutral under ongoing settler colonial regimes, its historical role having been to replace language, culture, community and values and to invade not just the land but also the bodies, including the mind and feelings, of the Indigenous people being colonized. This is reflected not just in the violent historical legacy of residential schools but also in the curricula and pedagogical approaches adopted in schools. Whose knowledge, whose pedagogical methodologies are used in schools where you live? Who is reflected in them? This seems like a good moment to introduce an educational stretch before proceeding much further.

Educational stretch: the impact of education on our understanding of gender

Take a moment to go back to the notes from the educational stretches in the previous chapters. You might still have the list or map from Chapter 3 as well as notes from Chapter 4. If you don't, it's ok. You can still engage with this activity. If you have your map and/or notes, take some time to view this through the lens of education. Are there stories about gender on your map or notes that you learned in schools or at any point in your engagement with the educational system? Are there places of blame and shame on the map/notes that come directly from experiences you have had in educational institutions? Whether you're referring to the map or notes created earlier, take a moment to notice what you have learned about gender in educational institutions. You may want to consider the following questions.

What did you learn about gender from textbooks in schools? You may want to consider history, geography, mathematics, social science, biology, chemistry, psychology, literature, philosophy, art, music and so on. What did you learn about gender from books in all the various disciplines you have come across in educational institutions? What did you learn about gender from your teachers, professors, principals, administrators and so on? Pay attention to what you learned both through their words and actions. What did you learn about gender from observing how teachers, professors, principals and administrators treated you and your peers? What did you learn about gender from participating in interactions with your peers in educational settings? You might want to take time to note in words, draw or explore through movement your answers to these questions.

Really take your time, if you can, with this activity. The more education you have participated in, the more types of educational institutions you might want to consider. Finally, what are the stories you learned in educational institutions that you still carry with you today? Once you are done with the activity, take time to breathe and take care of yourself in some way. It can be overwhelming to process how pervasive gender is in our lives if this is something you had not considered in depth before (and it can still be overwhelming, even if you have spent much of your life thinking about it).

From the educational stretch, you might have collected some of your own data about how education passes on colonial ideas of gender not just through the content taught, but also through the pedagogical approaches chosen, the interactions between teachers and school administrators and those between educators, administrators and students, as well as those amongst students themselves. Dominant models of education have been criticized for becoming pipelines to the prison-industrial complex for some, to the military complex for others, and to the ongoing reproduction of capitalism for almost everyone. Even higher education institutions, which theoretically might adopt a critical approach towards education, far too often reproduce the same epistemological discourses through the ways in which they work. For example, the knowledge produced might be critical of dominant models of education, but the ways in which higher education works perpetuate the same hierarchies and hegemonies we see in dominant culture. Colonial, capitalist, ableist, andronormative, cisheteronormative, racist values are sadly pervasive in all levels of education, thus facilitating the reproduction of the other systems already discussed here, including the mental health system, to which we turn next.

5.7 Mental health

Mental health and gender have a long history. As mentioned earlier, the very binary of sick/healthy can be viewed as inherently gendered and andronormative. Similarly, we could view the mad/sane binary as inherently gendered with sane being inherently andronormative, given that the baseline is not dissimilar to the one discussed in the section on medicine. In modern colonial history, madness is usually viewed as a sign of greatness in men and of hysteria and weakness in women. From the beginning then, mental health seems to be viewed as inherently about the exploration of deviance, weakness and hysteria in women.

Given that most of Freud's clients were young women, and that he is considered the father of therapy by most people, it is not surprising that women have been pathologized from the beginning in the history of psychotherapy. Freud, in fact, considered boys and men to be inherently moral and girls and women inherently amoral. Masculine morality was learned and upheld through fear of castration or emasculation, whereas girls and women are not guided by this fear and their morality is controlled by fathers first, then husbands. The stereotype, mentioned earlier, of girls and women as naturally manipulative, lying beings can be ascribed, in no small part, to Freud.

He also viewed lesbianism as dangerous in women because there would be no man to be responsible for their morality. Therefore lesbianism was seen as a potential portal into mental illness, whereas homosexuality in men was seen as neurosis but not as problematic, given that men are inherently moral beings. In Freud's views, lesbianism is the fault of the father and curable through psychoanalysis. Ironically, his brilliant daughter and close companion, Anna Freud, was a lesbian (see Sagan 1988).

It is probably not a shock then that there is so much stigma connected to mental health. After all, right from its psychoanalytic beginnings, mental illness was connected to amorality, a legacy that is challenging to distance ourselves from, and amorality was connected to femininity. Although we have come a long way, assumptions about the superiority of rationality persist in our field, at least within Anglo and Western dominant paradigms. For example, the field of cognitive behavioral therapy (CBT) rests on the assumption that we can literally exercise mind over matter. CBT does view a connection between thoughts, emotions and behaviors but mostly intervenes at the level of thoughts and behaviors, trying to change "distorted thinking" and "maladaptive behaviors." There is an almost unspoken assumption that "rational" thoughts and behaviors are always morally superior and to be preferred in the field of mental health.

It is no accident, in my opinion, that rational thoughts and behaviors are stereotypically associated with masculinity and, more specifically white and Anglo masculinity. Even though gender seems to be but a minor branch of topical interest in psychology and mental health, gendered assumptions run deep in our field. It's rare that anyone questions bold assertions, made by mental health providers on a daily basis, on how "men and women work." Those assumptions are, after all, foundational to many theories and approaches.

Even when gender is not mentioned at all in certain theories, in practice people tend to apply them differently with "male and female" clients. It's even rarer that the whole premise of two gender is put into question and, when it is, it only seems to pertain to transgender and/or nonbinary people, leaving the main tenets of gendered thinking in dominant culture untouched and unquestioned. Mental health with and for transgender and/or nonbinary people then becomes its own specialist branch, which means the rest of the field can continue undisturbed in their assumptions about men and women, as long as we keep to our turf and don't shake the cisgenderist foundation of the whole discipline. This too is a colonizing and capitalist approach. If we're kept separate from one another, we can be better controlled and, most importantly, there can be more specialties, and therefore more certifications and trainings to be sold and bought.

Even in the field of family therapy, where systemic thinking could open a different conversation about gender, all too often we fall back on established stereotypes and pseudoscience about gender as a rigid binary. Yet, I have found that when I can support people in connecting genuinely to gender as a historical, social and cultural construct, a better understanding of one another can emerge across differences that are made to look chasmic by people who are invested in selling solutions specific to "men," "women," and "transgender and/or nonbinary people." Unfortunately the discourse that men are from Mars, women are from Venus and trans people from Transylvania (at least according to *The Rocky Horror Picture Show*) is familiar to people and, like many other popular discourses, is reproduced effortlessly by providers and researchers who are also brought up within these dominant paradigms.

Sometimes people acknowledge that what they're working with are issues like toxic masculinity, but they're reluctant to then broaden the lens to indicate how larger systems support the reproduction of such harmful, colonial binaries. This means that, ironically, while working to dismantle toxic masculinity, they also keep reifying it by framing their work as being with "men" or "boys." I can understand how the latter is more marketable than the "smash the colonial patriarchy" approach I am proposing in this book but I truly believe that if we don't start questioning the rigidity of the gender binary altogether, for everyone, we will keep running around in circles to find ourselves in the same places, or maybe just a few inches over to the left. In the next chapter I address in more detail the proposed framework but, first, let's engage in one more clinical vignette.

Clinical vignette: managing erasure at work

"Robyn is tired of feeling unnoticed at work. No matter how hard they work, they seem to be overlooked for promotion, salary raises, training opportunities and so on. At the same time, they often feel tokenized when their company wants to demonstrate their commitment to diversity, given that their field is usually dominated by cis white men. Robyn's work is starting to suffer as they no longer feel motivated to do their best, given that nobody seems to notice. They have also been isolating from family and friends. Their spouse is concerned and has asked to go to family therapy with Robyn. They feel Robyn is no longer the person they married and they're starting to feel resentful of all the labor they do both at home and to take care of their two children. Robyn does not feel very invested in therapy but reluctantly agreed to attend after their spouse gave them an ultimatum of therapy or divorce. They are now in your therapy room."

Let's start with what, by now, might feel like familiar questions, such as who do you imagine Robyn to be? What is their gender, class, race, ethnicity, religion, citizenship and disability status, Indigeneity, social and economic status and so on? How about their spouse? What kind of job do you imagine Robyn to have? If you change any of these imagined characteristics, does the way you look at Robyn change? Do they feel like a reliable witness of the situation or do you question their experience at work and think there's a clinical issue going on? If you change the gender identity you imagine Robyn to be, does their credibility change or not?

Once you have explored this idea, take some time to reflect on what you believe your role as therapist might be. What do you see as your goal? Is it about helping Robyn to see that their spouse is hurting? Is it about making them more resilient so they don't feel so impacted by their job? Do you support them in developing the confidence of looking for a different job with a more supportive company, or to raise the issue with their boss? Do you decide to see Robyn individually, with their spouse, with their spouse and children or some combination thereof? What guides any of these choices for you? Do you feel you can relate to Robyn's story? If so, in what way? Where is the resonance for you? If not, why not? Where is the dissonance? How does resonating or not with Robyn's story impact the way you view this case? Once you have addressed the case clinically one way, can you imagine addressing it in a different way? Finally, what theoretical model and related interventions do you imagine using in a case like this? If you adopted a different theoretical model and related interventions, what might look different clinically and why?

Summary

- One of the most basic ways in which the law might reproduce a rigid gender binary is the legal definition of terms such as sex and gender. This is essential as many laws on sex and/or gender discrimination, depending on the country and chosen wording, might or might not protect trans people.
- Many of the historical legal issues about who can vote, own property or be recognized as having a certain nationality or belonging to a tribal nation are not just linked to gender but also to how we are racialized.
- One of the most heinous examples though of how the legal system perpetuates violence and oppression based on gender is the legal sterilization of disabled girls and women.
- Cis men dominate the field of politics by holding about three-quarters of all government representative positions, on a nearly global scale.
- People are criminalized and imprisoned in ways that continue to penalize Black, Brown, Indigenous, disabled, trans, queer, immigrant and sex workers' bodies in many countries.
- Constructions of femininity that hurt women in

courtrooms and in the penal system are those of femininity as "naturally" caring and maternal, or as manipulative, untrustworthy or circuitous.

- How spaces are conceived, designed, implemented and organized tells the stories of dominant discourses.

- Architectural design is often driven by inherent bias where the user is imagined to be cisgender, not disabled, and male. This is not surprising given both the male dominance in the field and the fact that most of the people commissioning architectural work are also men.

- The baseline in medicine is clearly the cisgender white male as evident in issues such as the lower level of knowledge, and/or public health investment, in reproductive and sexual health issues, transgender health issues, and cardiac issues in women, especially Black women.

- Disparities around gender and race clearly indicate who the medical system is failing: women, transgender people, queer people, Black people, Indigenous people, disabled people and people from lower income and educational backgrounds.

- There seems to be an inherent quality of hegemonic cisgenderist masculinity in the construction of health and healthy, as it pertains to the current state of medicine. This is unsurprising given the pervasive andronormativity in the field.

- Education can never be neutral under ongoing settler colonial regimes, its historical role having been to replace language, culture, community and values and to invade not just the land but also the bodies, including the mind and feelings, of the Indigenous people being colonized.

- There is an almost unspoken assumption that "rational" thoughts and behaviors are always morally superior and to be preferred in the field of mental health.
- Rigid binary assumptions of gender are foundational to many theories and approaches in the field of mental health.
- Even in the field of family therapy, where systemic thinking could open up a different conversation about gender, all too often we fall back on established stereotypes and pseudoscience about gender as a rigid binary.

CHAPTER 6

Towards healing

In the previous five chapters I explored the various ways in which a rigid gender binary is, first and foremost, part of the legacy of the ongoing settler colonial project. I illustrated how people of various identities and experiences are currently impacted, the role of intergenerational family trauma in perpetuating rigid gender binaries, and how these binaries play out in relationships and then in wider systems. I am aware that there are more issues, more impacts and more specific examples than I could possibly cover in one single book, without this becoming an encyclopedic tome. I hope you can forgive any omissions, knowing that those are my responsibility, and that this book might nonetheless be of use to you and your work.

In this final chapter, you will not find the educational stretches, thoughtful moments or clinical vignettes used in the previous ones, given that the focus is on practice. This whole chapter is dedicated to practices that promote the dismantling of a rigid gender binary, including gender essentialism and cisgenderism. This dismantling has to take place, not just behaviorally, but in our own very being. As such, it is one of the forms of neurodecolonizing—or decolonizing the mind—that Michael Yellow Bird invites us to engage in as practice (Wilson and Bird 2012). This follows the trail set by many, including Cordelia Fine, author of *Delusions of Gender* (2010), who highlights the connection between the way we/our brains work, and how we are shaped by environments and dominant culture.

I too want to highlight how many levels are involved in shedding colonial, rigid and binary ideas of gender. Therefore, I start the chapter with an invitation to examine your own relationship with this historical and biopsychosociocultural construct—gender—and highlight how reflective practices are pivotal in this work. After this, I discuss the role of dismantling of gendered assumptions, and the importance of engaging curiosity and irreverence as allies in this work. I also highlight how important it is to employ a trauma-informed approach at all stages; that is, an approach that is slow, kind and consensual. As part of this approach, I discuss the potential to challenge all/nothing thinking patterns in relation to gender, and to provide clients, students, learners or peers with resources and materials that make it possible for all of us to dream, envision and participate in collective healing from gendered trauma as we move forward together.

Much of what I discuss in this chapter is really about a politics of relationality. I have no idea of what the outcome will be, and I am definitely not trying to sell you a "healing from gendered trauma" (TM) technique. Ultimately, this is an invitation to move into a collective dance of liberation through the lens of gender.

6.1 Starting from our own gender(s): engaging reflective practices

As you read through this book, you might have noticed thoughts, emotions, sensations and reactions arise within you. These might have been familiar or unfamiliar thoughts. You might have experienced excitement, boredom, indifference, anger, frustration and any of the other reactions we are capable of as humans. Noticing what has been moved, if anything, in you might be a good starting place for this work.

This starting point is, in many ways, specific to you and yet there will be many others who also share it. If we imagine gender as a landscape, wherever you are, at this moment, in that landscape, is an excellent place to begin. Others might be there too, either at the same time, or they might have been there at another time. Nobody is alone in this journey, even though, far too often, we do not share this gender journey with others, unless invited or forced to do so because of our own social positioning. For example, Indigenous, Black and Brown people, disabled people, trans, nonbinary and queer people, as discussed throughout the book, might be forced to share their gender journey due to systemic and oppressive dynamics that do not impact other bodies in the same way.

Whoever you are and wherever you are, I invite you to take this as your starting point. If you haven't given gender much thought before this book, you might want to read an earlier book I co-authored with Meg-John Barker: *How to Understand Your Gender: A Practical Guide for Exploring Who You Are* (2018). That book was very much written for people who have not thought too much about gender before, although we have been told that many people who had thought about gender before also found it helpful.

Regardless of what your starting point might be, the practice recommended in this section is one of ongoing reflection. It might seem odd to recommend starting from reflection rather than action in a chapter focused on healing. However, I have found again and again that learning, understanding, changing, and ultimately hopefully healing, start from pausing and noticing. After all, in Anglo and other colonial cultures, we are often pushed to go fast, to act, to leap, to produce. Pausing, reflecting and noticing are not just trauma-informed, as I explore later, but also intrinsically counter-cultural, in many ways. In a world that tells us to go, go, go, what happens when we stop, hit the pause button and look around? We might just notice where we are and what's going on and have time to decide how to engage with it all.

First, let's take a moment to define what reflection is. Reflection can include looking back and looking forward. For example, in the case of the gender binaries discussed here, it might mean looking at where our understanding of gender has come from, as you have been invited to do throughout this book. Reflection is also about looking forward, to the future and potential actions and/or ongoing relationships. In this case, it might mean thinking about what you would like your relationship to gender to be moving forward. Are you satisfied with the way you relate to your own gender(s) and other people's gender(s)? How about the way in which other people relate to gender generally, and to your gender(s) more specifically?

Reflecting could therefore be described as starting where you are, to both look back and look forward. Looking back can be more focused on noticing, evaluating, assessing, sifting what we want to keep and bring forward with us, and what we want to leave in the past. Looking forward can be more about studying maps for the journey ahead, choosing a route, deciding how to best travel along that route, and thinking about when to stop and revise how the journey is going.

Reflection when it comes to gender can be vital as we are not, in dominant culture, encouraged to reflect on our own, or other people's, gender(s). In fact, quite the opposite is true. We are usually supposed to just go along with what other people tell us about our gender, and not question it, as much as possible. If we do question the way things work, we might be labelled early on as troublemakers, non-conforming and agitators of some kind.

This is something that even young children pick up on. Many trans and nonbinary people have described how they knew early on, as young as four or five years old, that talking about gender in ways that challenged the status quo was not acceptable. Teaching about gender since being a doctoral student and, at the time, 2nd-wave feminist, I also know how many stories of pain most people hold, regardless of their identities, when it comes to gender. There are stories about not being able to express feelings because of being assigned male at birth or being viewed as "ugly" because of not conforming to stereotypical beauty standards for those assigned female at birth. There are stories of not being able to play sports, wear what you want, being punished for how you sit, walk and talk, and who you hang out with. I am yet to meet someone who does not have at least one painful story when it comes to rigid gendered expectations. Reflection can help us pause, breathe, notice: how have we been impacted by these rigid gender binaries in the past? How are we impacted now? What relationship to gender do we want to cultivate and nurture moving forward?

If we do not pause and reflect, we keep perpetuating the same trauma, the same ways in which we were hurt, simply because we do not know that this is what we are doing. Feminist, scholar, author and activist Rachel Hare-Mustin spent much of her career writing about gender in psychotherapy. One of her seminal papers on "Discourses in the mirrored room" (1994) warns us that, if we do not pay attention, we end up reproducing the same systemic, dominant and oppressive discourses in places such as therapy rooms, which are supposed to be healing. This is why reflection is essential to this work of dismantling rigid gender binaries.

In dominant cultures, in which colonizers want us to believe that this is the way things have always been, reflection is the portal through which we can move and notice that this is simply untrue. There have been other ways, and there will be more ways in the future, because there are more ways of being right now. Reflections also enable us to see the smoke and mirrors for what they truly are. If we connect to our own stories and dissonances, and listen to those of others too, it becomes less and less possible to simply go along with the status quo, the way things are.

Whether you are a therapist, healer, educator or community organizer, it is likely that you use reflection in your own work. Reflection is often used to facilitate and deepen learning, to increase awareness of individual and relational patterns, and to review what has worked before so that we are not constantly starting from scratch.

In a way reflection was the source of this book. The deeper I delved into gender, over the past 25 years of academic work in this area, the more I realized that I could no longer talk about gender without talking about disability, citizenship, race, ethnicity, class and colonialism. What might change in your own work if you were to give yourself the space, permission and tools to delve deeper into gender in this way? Not just gender as an abstract concept, or as an engagement with genders other than yours, but as a reflective project of learning about yourself and your own gender journey so far? Do you have a map of your journey so far? If so, what difference does this make? If not, what possibilities might open up if you were to have your own personal gender map before engaging, or continuing to engage in this work with others?

Far too often, I have witnessed providers, educators and organizers have beautiful intentions but incredibly harmful impacts because of this lack of reflection. I truly believe that reflective practices can support us in reducing the potential for harm. We can never be completely safe for one another, and I am certainly not looking for a puritanical purity, which is in itself harmful. However, I think we can be more intentional, aware and kinder if we have done our own work, in any area, first.

What practices are there for reflection though? It seems simple to say that reflection is looking back and looking forward but that certainly does not provide enough tools. Reflective practices can vary a great deal. The building blocks are definitely pausing and noticing. We cannot reflect on anything if we are rushing along.

Reflection is, then, rooted in our capacity to be present. Cultivating presence is definitely more of a practice than a goal. We are continuously distracted from presence, even simply by our own thoughts. Practicing coming back, again and again, to right here, right now is the practice of presence. Some might call it mindfulness, but I prefer to stay with the more interdenominational idea of presence. How can staying present help us look back and look forward? Being present means knowing our baseline. As we reflect on gender, knowing our baseline means knowing where we are now in relationship to our own gender(s), the idea of gender and other people's genders. If we know our baseline, then we can more clearly notice what is in the past and what we might hope for in the future. We cannot do this without presence, or we might get lost in other memories or illusions.

There are several approaches to cultivating presence and, with this, increase our capacity for reflection. Mindfulness, as mentioned—an approach based in Buddhist traditions—is one of them. Other ways to cultivate presence and deepen our relationship with reflecting are:

- Journaling: the practice of writing down thoughts, feelings, memories, sensations and anything else we might want to notice. You could keep a "gender journal," for example, for a specific period of time, such as a week, month, season or a year. In this gender journal you could record observations, thoughts, memories, experiences and anything else you might like through the lens of gender. You can also use drawing, mind maps or collage in your journal.

- Sitting and thinking: you could simply choose to be with your thoughts and feelings about gender for a period of time. You could do this once or several times. This is a practice in which you cultivate your observer-self part to help you notice your own cognitive, emotional and relational patterns around gender.

- Wandering and wondering: similar to sitting and thinking but in motion. It could involve taking a walk, maybe even walking through a market or other populated areas to observe interactions through the lens of gender, making sure to focus on your own reactions to these interactions and owning your own stories about gender.

· Authentic movement: this is an expressive movement practice, started by Mary Starks Whitehouse in the 1950s as "movement in depth." It consists of a mover and witness usually. The mover moves according to an internal sense of movement, usually without music, while the witness observes their own reaction to watching the mover. There are groups globally engaging in this practice or you could do this with someone you know and trust, such as another provider and educator. You can move as you think about your own relationship with, and story of, gender and notice what emerges.

You can use any other technique, such as somatic observations, focusing and other practices developed to deepen our relationship with ourselves to reflect on gender, specifically your own gender journey so far, and what you would like that journey to be moving forward.

Reflecting does not need to be a solitary endeavor. John Burnham, for example, writes about *relational reflexivity* as a therapeutic and teaching tool. You can read more about John's work, if you like, if you follow up on the further reading for this chapter (Burnham 2005). At the heart, relational reflexivity is a way to ask questions about the process happening in the room, be it therapy or teaching and learning. Within this framework, you might want to invite a peer, or a small group of peers, to reflect on their gender journeys with you. You might all explore your understanding of gender together, your own gendered experiences so far, and how you would like to relate to gender, your own and other people's, moving forward. You could then, maybe during the last part of your discussion, reflect on the process itself.

John uses four quadrants in his model of relational reflexivity: resources, restraints, problems and possibilities. You might ask one another questions such as: What were the resources that emerged from our conversation on our gender journeys? What about the restraints? What problems have emerged in this conversation about gender, and what possibilities? You can also use this tool with clients or students at the later stages discussed in this chapter, of course.

No matter what tool you use for reflection, whether by yourself and/or with others, I encourage you to not bypass this stage before engaging in healing, teaching or organizing work with others around gender. This is your foundation that you can return to and revisit any time you need to. I know I have done so, and will continue to do so, many times as I keep engaging with this work. Reflective practices can be a powerful ally in our journey and enable us to not become stuck at one point in time and at a fixed understanding of gender.

6.2 From assumptions and stereotypes to irreverent curiosity

One of the things that reflecting can support us with, as providers, educators or organizers, is noticing how quickly we can make assumptions, if we are not careful. This is understandable, given what I mentioned about colonizing dominant cultures pushing us to go fast and not question anything much.

First, let's slow down and consider what assumptions and stereotypes are, and why we might want to avoid them.

Assumptions are things we decide about other people's identities and experiences without having all or any facts at our disposal. For example, someone might assume that I read a lot simply because I wear glasses. Stereotypes are fixed ideas held by large groups of people, usually within dominant culture, about other groups of people. A stereotype I have heard often, both in the UK and in North America, for example, is that Italians are loud and gesture a lot. Stereotypes can be based on aspects of truth but become stereotypes once they are applied indiscriminately to people without actually knowing them.

As humans, we are meaning-making animals and we want to make sense of things by being able to put them into categories. However, this does not work so well with other humans. When we place people into assumptions and stereotypes based on gender, for example, we deprive them of their full potential, to some degree, dehumanizing them. Assumptions and stereotypes sadly abound when it comes to gender.

I've mentioned, for example, more than once the typical "Men are from Mars and Women are from Venus" assumption, which, as you probably know by now, is one of my least favorite assumptions and stereotypes all in one. Not only is this stereotype not supported by most current science, but it also propagates dangerous assumptions about men and women, for example, the assumption that many people make about women being inherently incapable of reading maps, or men always being "up for sex."

More dangerous still is the assumption in dominant discourse that when women say "no" in relation to sex they mean "yes," an assumption visibly challenged by the #MeToo movement over the past few years. Or there is the assumption that "boys will be boys" that leads adults to leaving boys unsupervised, and often exposed to bullying and violence that has a lasting, deleterious impact in their lives.

Of course these stereotypes also reinforce the assumption that there are only two genders, as well as falling in line with cisheteronormative understandings and expectations of gender. Hopefully you understand how insidious, ubiquitous and harmful assumptions and stereotypes can be. Gender is, of course, but one aspect of possible assumptions and stereotypes, which can also be combined with racialized aspects of identities and experiences in incredibly oppressive and harmful ways.

Assumptions and stereotypes are certainly not conducive to trusting therapeutic, educational or community relationships. In fact they are often detrimental to people seeking therapeutic support, being able to learn or engaging with community organizing. All it takes is a harmful assumption or stereotype carelessly tossed into the room to undo trust, destroy any sense of safety and impede whatever rapport was hoped for.

You might think that maybe people "should be more resilient and less snowflakey." If that is one of the thoughts you are having right now, it makes sense. Dominant Anglo and colonial cultures thrive on individualistic ideas of strength, "grit" and "tough love." However, relational politics do not thrive in that soil. Relationships usually thrive in care, mutual respect, listening, understanding and openness. Assumptions and stereotypes close the door in the face of relationships. If someone slammed a door in your face, you'd expect them to apologize and do some repair, if this was a mistake. You would feel hurt by having a door slammed in your face, and rightly so. It is an unpleasant feeling. However, when it comes to assumptions and stereotypes, somehow we expect the person who just had the door of relationship slammed in their face to do all the work to open that door again. It just does not make sense. In fact, the less we can go around slamming metaphorical relational doors the better, especially if we work in caring, teaching or organizing fields.

As an antidote to assumptions and stereotypes, and towards better relationship building, I want to introduce two ideas from family therapy, specifically from the Milan School of Family Therapy: irreverence and curiosity. Cecchin, Lane and Ray (1993) wrote about irreverence at a time in family therapy when the tension between the roots of the field with cybernetics as an organizing metaphor and postmodern thinking was fairly high. In many ways, this tension was also about power, hierarchies and control within the therapy room. In the middle of these theoretical debates, these authors proposed that "therapists should maintain a *healthy disrespect* for any idea which restricts therapeutic maneuverability and creativity" (p.129). Inspired by Whitaker, they state that "thus the irreverent therapist fights the temptation of ever becoming a true believer in any approach or theory" (p.129).

Why am I revisiting the idea of irreverence here, when discussing assumptions and stereotypes? After all, irreverence might not seem the most obvious antidote, at first glance, to the perils of assumptions and stereotyping, and might even seem to enable them. However, I believe that irreverence, in the way that Cecchin and colleagues propose, can be quite a helpful concept here. What they are saying is not to place any theory above the actual relationship happening in the therapy room. To do so is to risk not being present and connected to what the family in the actual room might need from you as a therapist. Irreverence towards theoretical approaches, in this case, is about placing the therapeutic relationship in action above theoretical assumptions and, dare I say, stereotypes about how families, and therapy, are "supposed" to work.

The authors write: "To adopt a position of irreverence is to be slightly subversive against any reified 'truth.' If one begins to feel too committed to any belief system, one runs the risk of becoming instrumentalized" (p.129). For them this is about being engaged with the family, in the therapeutic moment, connected to them, following their own therapeutic instincts and where the family takes them. However, this is not an approach that eschews responsibility; they also write about irreverence that this "can only occur if we assume responsibility for our own actions, for our own opinions" (p.129).

Irreverence can help us move away from assumptions and stereotypes because we are essentially skeptical of any one approach to therapy, or any approach to education or community organizing. In this way, irreverence allows for a diversity of strategies to be employed in our work, something that is more consistent with politics of relationality, that is, where relationships come first. Interestingly Cecchin and colleagues also state that it is only with "continuous exercises in reflexivity (i.e., reflecting teams, discussions, etc.)" (p.133) that irreverence, as proposed, can truly work. Alongside reflexivity, curiosity is the other ingredient that needs to accompany irreverence, if this is to be an effective tool against assuming and stereotyping in our work. Curiosity, as stated by Cecchin in his paper revisiting some of the systemic principles adopted by the Milan School, "facilitates the development of multiplicity and polyphony. In this systemic orientation, we generate descriptions within a frame of curiosity rather than within a frame of true and false explanations" (Cechhin 1987, p.406).

Once more, curiosity is about opening up to multiplicity of experiences. This is something that, along with irreverence, I believe can be applied not just to therapeutic encounters but also to teaching, community organizing and general relationship building. I would say that to be irreverent of assumptions and stereotypes, no matter how embedded in a dominant culture, and to be curious is to be open to authentic connection and relationship.

When it comes to gender, being irreverent towards the idea of who I was "supposed" to be because of my sex assigned at birth, was personally an antidote to assumptions and stereotypes I had absorbed, and allowed me to explore who I am. In this ongoing becoming, I came to my own identity. As a therapist, I have also experienced supporting clients and their families in their own becoming, wherever this might lead them (and often their journey is very different from mine).

With irreverence and curiosity as my guides, I have been able to gently ask questions that might feel otherwise impossible, such as "do you believe to be trans is to be sick?" to clients who were struggling with internalized pathologization and transphobia. These are not easy questions to ask, yet in those relational moments, I can connect and say, "I see what you are struggling with, it makes sense, given the world we live in. Is this what you truly believe? Is this where you want to stay?" and then open up to explore where they might want to go.

I have also been able to propose to cishetero couples "queer solutions" to their "straight problems," for example, gently and irreverently encouraging them to examine what they have learned about masculinity and femininity, and to consider whether this is serving them in their actual relationship, or exploring whether they're trying to live up to stereotypes and assumptions that serve only the dominant culture and the reproduction of oppressive relational dynamics.

These are, of course, tools to hold with open hands, making sure, as Cecchin and colleagues remind us, to engage in ongoing reflective practices to make sure we are doing no harm. In some ways, when we do so, we move towards unexplored territories with our clients, students, peers and communities. We dare to open to possibility, to new stories of gender, and more.

6.3 Kind, slow, consensual and embodied: a trauma-informed approach

What do I mean by holding these tools with open hands? I mean to hold them lightly, picking them up and putting them down as needed. I learned this expression from my friend and writing partner, Meg-John Barker, who found the following quote by Buddhist teacher Martine Batchelor about holding things with open hands:

> Let's imagine that I am holding an object made of gold. It is so precious and it is mine – I feel I must hold onto it. I grasp it, curling my fingers so as not to drop it, so that nobody can take it away from me. What happens after a while? Not only do my hand and arm get cramp but I cannot use my hand for anything else. When you grip something, you create tension and limit yourself.
>
> Dropping the golden object is not the solution. Non-attachment means learning to relax to uncurl the fingers and gently open the hand. When my hand is wide open and there is no tension, the precious object can rest lightly on my palm. I can still value the object and take care of it; I can put it down and pick it up; I can use my hand for doing something else. (Batchelor and Batchelor 2001, p.96)

Much of what I am suggesting in this final chapter needs to be held with open hands. After all, not everything will work for and with everyone. I also truly believe that it is ok to hold the construct of gender itself with open hands. When we can do so, there is hopefully much more expansiveness for all identities and experiences.

Given also that I am framing a rigid gender binary as part of historical, cultural and social trauma, it is important to take a moment to explore further what it means to take a trauma-informed approach to dismantling cisgenderism. I want to be clear that I still support a diversity of tactics when it comes to dismantling any colonial legacies, including a rigid gender binary, and I also believe that healing needs to be rooted in trauma-informed, liberatory approaches.

In the title to this section, I have used the words kind, slow, consensual and embodied. This is the approach I want to discuss here.

What do I mean by "kind" when it comes to gender? Much of the gendered trauma discussed in this book is rooted in rigid, harsh policing of our bodies, our movements, even our thoughts about gender. To take a kind approach to gender is, then, inherently counter to the gendered violence that continues to be imposed on our bodies in a variety of ways. Kind does not mean non-confrontational. In fact, sometimes, the kind thing to do is to confront others when they are doing harm to themselves and others. For example, if someone is forcing themselves to fit into a rigid stereotype of masculinity, femininity or androgyny, because they think this is what other people want, then the kind approach would be to highlight this, and to explore why they feel compelled to do so. Is this for safety, which is an absolutely legitimate concern, or is this out of not being aware of any other options? I discuss further how some people might fall into the trap of all/nothing polarized thinking when it comes to gender in the next section. For now, suffice to say that kind does not mean soft, or rolling over in the face of oppression, but rather it means compassionate, vulnerable and open.

This is where having done our own work on gender is essential. If we have done that, we can be much more open and vulnerable about how hard it can be to challenge cisheteronormative expectations of gender. If we are at peace with our own gender and feel no need to police our bodies in harsh, colonial and controlling ways, then we do not need to do this with other people either.

Kindness is, of course, just like any of the other approaches described here: only possible when we are not immersed into a trauma response, that is, fight, flight, freeze or fawn (people pleasing for survival). This is the foundation of doing our own work. If we do not, we risk coming from a place of reactivity and survival, which often leads to more trauma and, ultimately, more violence towards ourselves and others. Being kind, in this context, then, means not being reactive but rather noticing where the other person or people are at and being able to meet them there with clarity about ourselves and what we believe in.

For example, in my spiritual tradition, over the summer of 2018 there was some upheaval about some statements made by one of the founders about supporting a well-known trans-exclusionary radical feminist Pagan leader. Being kind, in this context, meant, for me, being very publicly clear on the direction of the harm happening: the ongoing, historical transmisogyny in many Pagan and Goddess-related traditions. I am sure some of my statements were not seen as kind depending on who was reading them, but, for me, kindness was sitting with what had been said, reflecting on it, being clear on the historical context, and also on the direction of the harm perpetuated, including an ability to distinguish harm from discomfort or from entitlement to a public platform. We can be kind and still name harm when this happens. Eventually the incident led a group of us, in the bioregion where I live, to write a collective statement that many other community members, globally, decided to co-sign.

I mentioned sitting with what had been said in the example above. This meant not responding immediately, on the same day, despite the urgency many felt around the issue. The statement too emerged several weeks after the initial incident, once we had time to interact, engage, witness one another struggle, organize and connect. All of this took time, which is why I named "slow" as another component of a trauma-informed approach. Slow does not mean immobile, of course; it just means not having a knee-jerk reaction. Slow, as mentioned earlier, is essential to reflective practices. We cannot rush and reflect usually! We can also not reflect when we are in the middle of a survival response.

I am aware that to be able to be slow, kind and reflective takes a lot of privilege, which is why I think much more could be accomplished in our struggle for gender liberation if people with privilege in this area could be more engaged. However, the reality is that, even in the middle of struggling for survival, many trans and/or nonbinary people, especially trans feminine people of color, have taken the time to openly, compassionately and vulnerably share their own relationships with gender. This includes Laverne Cox, Janet Mock, Andrea Jenkins and Carmen Carrera, just to name a few contemporary, well-known figures.

All of these people used their relative privilege—compared to people with larger systemic power, such as cis white people in the US context specifically—and took their time to educate people about gender, as well as the intersection of transness, femininity and race. What I have witnessed again and again is people who are most impacted by this rigid, colonial gender binary being patient—that is slow, kind and vulnerable—when approaching gender. I have also witnessed, far too often, people with considerable privilege when it comes to gender, as well as race, being quick to judge, unwilling to listen and fast to armor and harm.

These are, of course, generalizations and, as always, there are exceptions to this picture. However, when it comes to gender, if you are having a knee-jerk reaction of some kind, what becomes possible if you slow down and—with curiosity—investigate where that reaction is coming from, especially if you have relative privilege in this area?

This can be hard if you feel attacked, of course, but pausing and slowing down can also help us view more clearly whether we are being attacked or feel attacked. For example, I have had conversations with cis white feminists who hold a lot of pain when it comes to gender and who struggle to see their own transmisogyny because their pain is literally obfuscating the reality of their actions and impact. Being able to slow down with them, sometimes, if they are willing to truly listen, can lead to an opening where we can see that our struggles are connected, that there is no hierarchy of oppression, that we do not need to be pitted against one another. If we slow down, it also becomes harder for colonial, conservative forces to manipulate us by stoking the flames of our trauma and blowing smoke around, making us think we are each other's enemies, until we are so confused that we end up in alliances we never thought possible or desirable. Going slow helps us reflect, notice where we are going and be intentional, which, in turn, makes it more possible to also be consensual, another tenet of trauma-informed practices.

What does "consent" have to do with gender? Quite a lot in

the context of gendered trauma given that, at the heart of the latter, is often a lack of consent. This could be a non-consensual gendering into a binary of people and gender identities and roles that colonizers did not understand, or the non-consensual violence perpetrated against femme people of all genders.

If we are to move towards healing gendered trauma then consent needs to be at the heart of our practices and relationships. Consent needs to also be understood as much larger than just in the sexual arena. For example, in many dominant cultures, children are often treated non-consensually, starting from the very practice of assigning them a gender at birth, which if inaccurate can lead to significant harm. Even when accurate, this leads to the closing down of so many possibilities from a young age. Non-consensual gendering of children still in the womb is so commonplace that even popular TV shows, which are otherwise fairly socially and politically conscious, such as *This Is Us* in the US, portray practices such as "gender reveal parties" without any critical engagement. The latter practice is particularly ironic, given that the blogger and mother who started gender reveal parties then asked for people to stop engaging in this practice after their child came out as nonbinary.

Keeping consent central to the healing from gendered trauma is, therefore, another antidote to all those moments of individual, cultural, social and historical violence. It is about recognizing how much violence has already been perpetrated in larger and more visible ways, as well as in hidden ways, that might seem small but are no less harmful to the people impacted.

Consent, to be effective, though, needs to include a critical and ongoing analysis of power. For example, some cis people have often complained that they are being called "cis" without having "consented" to it. This is disingenuous, as they are taking a systemic issue, cisgenderism, and the original, othering labeling of "trans" without the labeling of its counterpart "cis," and then applying an individual model of consent to this systemic issue: that is, "I, as an individual, did not consent to be labelled as cis." Cis, as a label, was created to make the point that if we label some people as trans, then we need to have a label for those people whose sex assigned at birth aligns with their gender identity. Given that trans is a Latin prefix meaning across, using the Latin prefix cis, to signify on the same side of, seemed appropriate. To then take a response to systemic oppression, such as the creation of the label cis, and individualize it, even through the lens of consent, is inappropriate unless, of course, the person being labeled identifies as trans and/or nonbinary but then it's another issue altogether.

In this example, it's an individual applying a micro lens to a macro problem. Ultimately, approaching gender consensually is about not using any singular gender identities or experiences as a weapon. In the 1980s, UK feminists Stanley and Wise mentioned that, if the personal truly is political, then we cannot discount any personal experiences as apolitical, including those of "ordinary naff heterosexual men" (1983/2002, p.18). Approaching gender consensually therefore is about no longer weaponizing gender, in any direction. This can be incredibly challenging to do when people with certain identities and experiences have been harmed so much more than others. However, it is only through stopping perpetuating the use of gender identities and expressions as weapons that we can start moving towards collective healing.

This might all seem rather intellectual and I want to take a moment to recognize that we cannot truly adopt a trauma-informed approach without considering humans as "embodied" beings, both individually and collectively. Even though I am trying to translate into words some of the ways in which I and others work towards our gender liberation, this is in many ways challenging as the work is deeply embodied. If this work of healing and gender liberation starts within, as pointed out in section 6.1, then we cannot do this work purely from a cognitive perspective. I did not wake up one morning and decide I was trans and nonbinary. I had to put together a series of feelings, experiences, thoughts and sensations and then found labels that explained some of them. However, the yearning to work for collective gender liberation runs deeper and it's almost harder to articulate in words, although I have taken many, many words in this book to try and explore with you.

This yearning, for me, is much more akin to what disabled, mestiza author, organizer and activist Naomi Ortiz describes as "critical-feeling," a form of:

> emotionally reaching out to the world… It's moving beyond facts and information that we logically learn through words and ideas. I become aware of feelings where there are little or no words to describe their purpose. It is this awareness, this risk to inexplicably feel, that allows me to pull energy inward. (Ortiz 2018, p.39)

Naomi talks about this in the context of self-care, and our capacity to identify our needs in relation to this. I know when I started to sense the dissonance between what the world told me about gender and what my experience was, this critical-feeling is what allowed me to stay present with myself, despite the pressure to disappear into an easy binary category. I include it here because as you do this work and maybe even support others in doing this work, there might be somatic experiences—critical-feeling—before there can be words. In my experience, if we can allow space for those experiences and feelings, the words and knowledge might eventually come too.

6.4 Approaching the male/female binary as an all/nothing pattern

How can we move through this critical-feeling and find a way to healing from gendered trauma when we are immersed in such binary, rigid and polarizing thinking about gender at every turn, as illustrated in this book? A reminder I find helpful is that trauma, especially developmental trauma, often shapes our thinking into this polarity, this all/nothing, pink/blue, man/woman. When I view the rigidity of this binary through this lens, I can also be more compassionate towards myself and others when we get caught in its net.

All/nothing patterns are tough to break out of, after all. We can notice the rigidity of the gender binary in a range of ways: the gendering of chromosomes, body parts, behaviors, mannerisms, clothing, emotions, toys, experiences, and so on. All/nothing thinking patterns are those that view duality as the only option. For example: you are male or female, good or bad, with us or against us. Given that we live in a cloud of historical, intergenerational, cultural and social trauma when it comes to gender, it makes sense that we have internalized much of this thinking.

In fact, even when we get away from binary ideas of gender, we might still engage in all/nothing thinking patterns, if we are not careful. For example, some young people who identify as trans and/or nonbinary have internalized such a deep need to police gender that they might be afraid of being viewed as "trans trenders" (that is people who think they are trans because it's "trendy"). Within this paradigm, you are trans or not (another all/ nothing pattern). There is no exploring, playing or considering; there is simply, you are or you are not. Some trans and cis people alike question the validity of nonbinary genders, and then other trans and/or nonbinary people turn around and talk about "truscum," that is, those trans people who align with a medicalized and pathologizing model of gender and believe that dysphoria is an essential trait for some people.

All/nothing patterns are insidious and, if we are not careful, we tend to reproduce the same discourses that oppressed us, creating and recreating boundaries around gender identities and experiences to make sure we know who is "in" and who is "out," who is "with us" and who is "against us." While these patterns are understandable, when people are hurt, in survival mode and trying to protect themselves, this is not conducive to healing or liberation. As long as there is policing of gender, any gender, there cannot truly be liberation. This is a really tough one for many of us who have been hurt by rigid gender binaries, and who might have come to our identities through hardship, risk and loss. It is so tempting to feel that now that we are "in," whichever label, identity or experience that "in" might be, we get to police others and make sure that "fakers" and "trenders" are kept out.

We are simply afraid. Afraid that if we let anyone in who is not 100 percent certain, or in agreement with us, or just like us, we might get hurt. We are afraid that whatever we have built will be blown away. It is understandable. It is what everyone is afraid of. Trauma keeps us afraid of one another. Colonial and patriarchal ways of thinking divide us, and seduce us into believing that, if we behave in certain ways, we too could have power over our little domain, whatever that domain might be. However, these are all lies, lies that trauma tells us and that oppression thrives on. These dualities of Men are from Mars and Women from Venus, cis women against trans women, sex workers versus SWERFs (sex worker exclusive radical feminists) are all deeply rooted in historical, cultural and social trauma.

How can we, then, find another way? The idea of another way is key. If polarities are foundational to all/nothing patterns, our way to liberation can only be found in a third road. Building and nurturing flexibility in our individual and collective soma (bodies) is therefore key. Practicing saying and noticing the maybe, the pause between breathing in and breathing out, reflection, curiosity, slow, kind and consensual relationships are key to healing. We cannot heal from gendered trauma when we are still caught in rigid polarities, still invested in finding a perpetrator or savior so that we can stay in a victim place. Or so invested in being the irredeemable perpetrator that there is no hope for us. Once more, it starts with us, our own gender journey and dismantling internalized polarities first.

Once we engage with this work, we can then support those around us—be they clients, students, fellow community members and communities—to challenge those polarities within themselves and one another. This might all seem very idealistic, and it is. I truly believe we cannot move towards healing through violence. If we are to heal from gendered trauma it has to be through relationships: human, messy, complicated, infuriating, joyful, loving relationships. We cannot be in relationship when we are in opposition. We can be in a tug of war, push and pull at one another but, as long as we stay locked into these patterns, we can only view ourselves as victors and losers. In the meantime, the only victors seem to be systems of oppression. Can it truly be as simple as that, as helping ourselves and others be in better relationships? As simple as a naive John Lennon song? Or is this just another neo-liberal dream of unity? You might be disappointed to learn that I have no firm answers for you at this point, only questions and fragments and an invitation to participate in visioning a decolonial understanding of gender.

6.5 Collective dreams, visions and possibilities

What is, though, a decolonial understanding of gender? We cannot bathe in the same river twice: I don't believe that we can go back to a mythical, pre-colonial past. We cannot erase history, trauma, and just pretend it never happened/ is still happening. As a trauma therapist I witness these desires on an individual basis almost daily. So many of my clients wish to just forget, pretend whatever happened did not happen, or think that eradicating the perpetrator in some way might bring peace. However, when there has been a wound, the wound needs to be tended to. It needs to be noticed, cleaned and treated and it takes time to heal. What would a pre-colonial past even look like for many of us who were involuntarily or voluntarily displaced in a number of ways, including due to gendered violence? I think that comfort and connection can be found in the past but I am not so sure that our future can be found there.

I have written elsewhere (see further reading) that to think about the future directions of nonbinary genders is science fiction and a number of much better authors than I have engaged, and continue to engage, in those questions. I do know that healing from gendered trauma is a landscape that I do not know if we can even begin to imagine. However, it is a critical-feeling of a possibility that has not come to be yet. I sense into it when I am around other people who actively challenge normative ideas of gender in favor of authenticity, no matter what their own gender identities and experiences might be. I taste it when I am in communities where consent, healing and relationships are at the center: the heart of what we are doing. I smell it in the wind of younger generations who, often, no longer think like us when it comes to gender, but are still shaped and impacted by our trauma.

I believe that healing from gendered trauma lives in the spaces between us: the spaces across which we try to reach for one another when we dream of community, when we create structures centered around healing justice and liberation, when we strive for disability justice and access, when we dare to envision inclusive spaces. There is no definitive answer here, no listicle I can give you, or magic formula for how to fix the painful impact of this historical, cultural, intergenerational and social trauma of a rigid gender binary. However, I believe that if we can start to notice the wound, engage with it critically, start to clean it up within and between ourselves, we can start to plant seeds for another world of possibilities. This is a world in which we are connected to the past, where we do not deny or erase our history, but do not get stuck in it; rather we move forward reclaiming what is ours, and creating anew what was destroyed. This book is a long, open-handed invitation to this dream of gender liberation for our collective healing. How will you respond?

Further reading, references and resources

Chapter 1

Ansara, Y.G. and Hegarty, P. (2012). 'Cisgenderism in psychology: Pathologising and misgendering children from 1999 to 2008.' *Psychology & Sexuality*, 3, 2, 137–160.

Ansara, Y. G. and Hegarty, P. (2014). 'Methodologies of misgendering: Recommendations for reducing cisgenderism in psychological research.' *Feminism & Psychology*, 24, 2, 259–270.

Aizura, A.Z. (Ed.) (2014). *Decolonizing the Transgender Imaginary*. Durham, NC: Duke University Press.

Atwood, M. (1985/1996). *The Handmaid's Tale*. London: Vintage.

Bem, S. (1993). 'Introduction.' *In The Lenses of Gender: Transforming the Debate on Sexual Inequality*. New Haven, CT: Yale University Press.

binaohan, b. (2014). *Decolonizing Trans/Gender 101*. Biyuti Publishing.

Blumer, M.L., Gavriel Ansara, Y. and Watson, C.M. (2013). 'Cisgenderism in family therapy: How everyday clinical practices can delegitimize people's gender self-designations.' *Journal of Family Psychotherapy*, 24, 4, 267–285.

Brave Heart, M.Y.H., Chase, J., Elkins, J. and Altschul, D.B. (2011). 'Historical trauma among indigenous peoples of the Americas: Concepts, research, and clinical considerations.' *Journal of Psychoactive Drugs*, 43, 4, 282–290.

Dunbar-Ortiz, R. (2014). *An Indigenous Peoples' History of the United States* *(Vol. 3)*. Boston, MA: Beacon Press.

Eyers, P. (2017). 'Decolonization – meaning what exactly?' Accessed on 07/02/2020 at https://unsettlingamerica.wordpress.com/2017/10/11/ decolonization-meaning-what-exactly

Fausto-Sterling, A. (2008). *Myths of Gender: Biological Theories about Women and Men.* New York: Basic Books.

Fine, C. (2010). *Delusions of Gender: The Real Science behind Sex Differences.* London: Icon Books Ltd.

Gray, J. (1992). *Men Are from Mars, Women Are from Venus: A Practical Guide for Improving Communication and Getting What You Want in Your Relationships.* New York: HarperCollins Publishers.

Harriot, M. (2019). 'Republicans, men and Christians aren't trying to ban abortions: white people are.' *The Root.* Accessed on 07/02/2020 at www.theroot.com/ republicans-men-and-christians-arent-trying-to-ban-abo-1834820971

Heart, B. and Horse, M.Y. (2000). 'Wakiksuyapi: Carrying the historical trauma of the Lakota.' *Tulane Studies in Social Welfare*, 21, 22, 245–266.

Iantaffi, A. and Barker, M.J. (2018). *How to Understand Your Gender: A Practical Guide for Exploring Who You Are.* London: Jessica Kingsley Publishers.

Iantaffi, A., Barker, M.J., van Anders, S. and Scheele, J. (2019). Mapping Your Sexuality: From sexual orientation to sexual configuration theory. Accessed on 09/02/2020 at www.rewriting-the-rules.com/wp-content/ uploads/2018/08/MappingYourSexuality.pdf

Indigenous Action (2014). 'Accomplices not allies: Abolishing the ally industrial complex.' Accessed on 07/02/2020 at www.indigenousaction. org/accomplices-not-allies-abolishing-the-ally-industrial-complex

Lorde, A. (ed.) (1984/2007). 'The Master's Tools Will Never Dismantle the Master's House.' In *Sister Outsider: Essays and Speeches.* Berkeley, CA: Crossing Press.

Rippon, G. (2019). *The Gendered Brain: The New Neuroscience that Shatters the Myth of the Female Brain.* London: Bodley Head.

Saini, A. (2017). *Inferior: How Science Got Women Wrong—and the New Research That's Rewriting the Story.* Boston, MA: Beacon Press.

Snorton, C.R. (2017). *Black on Both Sides: A Racial History of Trans Identity*. Minneapolis, MN: University of Minnesota Press.

Sotero, M. (2006). 'A conceptual model of historical trauma: Implications for public health practice and research.' *Journal of Health Disparities Research and Practice, 1,* 1, 93–108.

Tuck, E. and Wayne Yang, K. (2012). 'Decolonization is not a metaphor.' *Decolonization: Indegeneity, Education & Society, 1,* 1, 1–40. Accessed on 07/02/2020 at https://jps.library.utoronto.ca/index.php/des/article/view/18630/15554

Veracini, L. (2015). *The Settler Colonial Present*. London: Palgrave Macmillan.

Wilson, W.A. and Bird, M.Y. (2012). *For Indigenous Minds Only: A Decolonization Handbook*. Sante Fe, NM: School for Advanced Research Press.

Wollstonecraft, M. (1792/2020). *A Vindication of the Rights of Woman*. London: Penguin.

Chapter 2

Anzaldúa, G. (1987). *Borderlands/La Frontera: The New Mestiza* (Vol. 3). San Francisco, CA: Aunt Lute.

Baral, S.D., Poteat, T., Strömdahl, S., Wirtz, A.L., Guadamuz, T.E. and Beyrer, C. (2013). 'Worldwide burden of HIV in transgender women: A systematic review and meta-analysis.' *The Lancet Infectious Diseases, 13,* 3, 214–222.

Bem, S.L. (1983). 'Gender schema theory and its implications for child development: Raising gender-aschematic children in a gender-schematic society.' *Signs: Journal of Women in Culture and Society, 8,* 4, 598–616.

Bem, S.L. (1993). *The Lenses of Gender: Transforming the Debate on Sexual Inequality*. New Haven, CT: Yale University Press.

Bertakis, K.D., Azari, R., Helms, L.J., Callahan, E.J. and Robbins, J.A. (2000). 'Gender differences in the utilization of health care services.' *Journal of Family Practice, 49,* 2, 147–147.

Carver, P.R., Yunger, J.L. and Perry, D.G. (2003). 'Gender identity and adjustment in middle childhood.' *Sex Roles, 49,* 95–109.

Collins, P.H. and Bilge, S. (2016). *Intersectionality*. Cambridge: Polity Press.

Crenshaw, K. (1989). 'Demarginalizing the intersection of race and sex: A black feminist critique of antidiscrimination doctrine, feminist theory, and antiracist politics.' *Feminism and Politics*, 314–343.

Crenshaw, K. (1990). 'Mapping the margins: Intersectionality, identity politics, and violence against women of color.' *Stanford Law Review*, 43, 6, 1241–1299.

Crenshaw, K. (forthcoming). *On Intersectionality: Essential Writings*. New York: The New Press.

Dean, M.L. and Tate, C.C. (2017). 'Extending the legacy of Sandra Bem: Psychological androgyny as a touchstone conceptual advance for the study of gender in psychological science.' *Sex Roles*, 76, 11–12, 643–654.

Egan, S.K. and Perry, D.G. (2001). 'Gender identity: A multidimensional analysis with implications for psychological adjustment.' *Developmental Psychology*, 17, 451–463.

Flanders-Stepans, M.B. (2000). 'Alarming racial differences in maternal mortality.' *The Journal of Perinatal Education*, 9, 2, 50.

Fredericks B., Daniels C., Judd, J., Bainbridge, R. *et al.* (2017). *Gendered Indigenous Health and Wellbeing within the Australian Health System: A Review of the Literature*. Rockhampton: CQUniversity, Australia.

Grant, J.M., Mottet, L.A., Tanis, J., Harrison, J., Herman, J.L. and Keisling, M. (2011). *Injustice at Every Turn: A Report of the National Transgender Discrimination Survey*. Washington: National Center for Transgender Equality and National Gay and Lesbian Task Force. Accessed on 04/02/2020 at www.transequality.org/sites/default/files/docs/resources/NTDS_Report.pdf

Hoffman, K.M., Trawalter, S., Axt, J.R. and Oliver, M.N. (2016). 'Racial bias in pain assessment and treatment recommendations, and false beliefs about biological differences between blacks and whites.' *Proceedings of the National Academy of Sciences*, 113, 16, 4296–4301.

hooks, b. (1981/2014). *Ain't I a Woman: Black Women and Feminism*. New York: Routledge.

hooks, b. (1989). *Talking Back: Thinking Feminist, Thinking Black*. Boston, MA: South End Press.

Hunt, S. (2016). *An Introduction to the Health of Two-Spirit People: Historical, Contemporary and Emergent Issues.* Prince George, BC: National Collaborating Centre for Aboriginal Health.

Hutchinson, D.L. (2000). 'Identity crisis: Intersectionality, multidimensionality, and the development of an adequate theory of subordination.' *Michigan Journal of Race and Law, 6,* 285.

Iantaffi, A. and Bockting, W.O. (2011). 'Views from both sides of the bridge? Gender, sexual legitimacy and transgender people's experiences of relationships.' *Culture, Health & Sexuality, 13, 3,* 355–370.

Iantaffi, A. (2015). 'Gender and Sexual Legitimacy.' *Current Sexual Health Reports, 7, 2,* 103–107.

James, S.E., Herman, J.L., Rankin, S., Keisling, M., Mottet, L. and Anafi, M. (2016). *The Report of the 2015 U.S. Transgender Survey.* Washington, DC: National Center for Transgender Equality.

Juster, R.P., Pruessner, J.C., Desrochers, A.B., Bourdon, O. *et al.* (2016). 'Sex and gender roles in relation to mental health and allostatic load.' *Psychosomatic Medicine, 78, 7,* 788–804.

Lester, C.N. (2018). *Trans Like Me: Conversations for All of Us.* New York: Seal Press.

Liben, L.S. and Bigler, R.S. (2017). 'Understanding and undermining the development of gender dichotomies: The legacy of Sandra Lipsitz Bem.' *Sex Roles, 76,* 9–10, 544–555.

Lucchesi, A. and Echo-Hawk, A. (2018). *Missing and Murdered Indigenous Women & Girls: A snapshot of data from 71 urban cities in the United States.* Seattle, WA: Urban Indian Health Institute. Accessed on 04/02/2020 at www.uihi.org/wp-content/uploads/2018/11/Missing-and-Murdered-Indigenous-Women-and-Girls-Report.pdf

Maher, F.A. and Tetreault, M.K. (1993). 'Frames of positionality: Constructing meaningful dialogues about gender and race.' *Anthropological Quarterly,* 118–126.

Morris, J. (1991). *Pride against Prejudice: Transforming Attitudes to Disability.* London: The Women's Press.

O'Neal, L. (2018). 'The struggle is real: The unrelenting weight of being a Black, female athlete,' *The Undefeated*. Accessed on 09/02/2020 at https://theundefeated.com/features/the-struggle-is-real-the-unrelenting-weight-of-being-a-black-female-athlete

Pierce, A. (2009). *Shattered Hearts: The Commercial Sexual Exploitation of American Indian Women and Girls in Minnesota*. Minneapolis, MN: Minnesota Indian Women's Resource Center. Accessed on 04/02/2020 at www.niwrc.org/sites/default/files/documents/Resources/Shattered-Hearts-Full.pdf

Poteat, T., Scheim, A., Xavier, J., Reisner, S. and Baral, S. (2016). 'Global epidemiology of HIV infection and related syndemics affecting transgender people.' *Journal of Acquired Immune Deficiency Syndromes, 72* (Suppl 3), S210–S219.

Rose, G. (1997). 'Situating knowledges: positionality, reflexivities and other tactics.' *Progress in Human Geography, 21, 3*, 305–320.

Russell, L. (2010). *Fact sheet: Health disparities by race and ethnicity*. Center for American Progress, 9. Accessed on 09/02/2020 at www.americanprogress.org/issues/healthcare/news/2010/12/16/8762/fact-sheet-health-disparities-by-race-and-ethnicity

Sacks, T.K. (2019). *Invisible Visits: Black Middle-Class Women in the American Healthcare System*. New York: Oxford University Press.

Sanchez, D.T. and Crocker, J. (2005). 'Why investment in gender ideals affects well-being: The role of external contingencies of self-worth.' *Psychology of Women Quarterly 29*, 63–77.

Sanchez, D.T., Crocker, J. and Boike, K.R. (2005). 'Doing gender in the bedroom: Investing in gender norms and the sexual experience.' *Personality and Social Psychology Bulletin 31*, 1445– 55.

Serano, J. (2007/2016). *Whipping girl: A Transsexual Woman on Sexism and the Scapegoating of Femininity*. Berkeley, CA: Seal Press.

Serano, J. (2013). *Excluded: Making Feminist and Queer Movements More Inclusive*. Berkeley, CA: Seal Press.

Sidanius, J. and Pratto, F. (1999/2001). *Social Dominance: An Intergroup Theory of Social Hierarchy and Oppression*. Cambridge: Cambridge University Press.

Stevens, J.A., Ballesteros, M.F., Mack, K.A., Rudd, R.A., DeCaro, E. and Adler, G. (2012). 'Gender differences in seeking care for falls in the aged Medicare population.' *American Journal of Preventive Medicine*, 43, 1, 59–62.

Walker, A. (2011). 'Coming Apart: By Way of Introduction to Lorde, Teish and Gardner.' In *You Can't Keep a Good Woman Down*. Open Road Media.

Chapter 3

Braga, L.L., Mello, M.F. and Fiks, J.P. (2012). 'Transgenerational transmission of trauma and resilience: A qualitative study with Brazilian offspring of Holocaust survivors.' *BMC Psychiatry*, 12, 1, 134.

Degruy-Leary, J. (1994/2005). *Post-Traumatic Slave Syndrome: America's Legacy of Enduring Injury*. Portland, OR: Joy DeGruy Publications Inc.

Fromm, G. (Ed.) (2012/2018). *Lost in Transmission: Studies of Trauma across Generations*. Abingdon: Routledge.

Gray, J. (2003). *Mars and Venus in the Bedroom: A Guide to Lasting Romance and Passion*. London: Random House.

Hicks, S.R. (2015). 'A Critical Analysis of Post Traumatic Slave Syndrome: A Multigenerational Legacy of Slavery.' Doctoral dissertation, California Institute of Integral Studies.

Hoosain, S. (2013). 'The Transmission of Intergenerational Trauma in Displaced Families.' Unpublished thesis.

Hulette, A.C., Kaehler, L.A. and Freyd, J.J. (2011). 'Intergenerational associations between trauma and dissociation.' *Journal of Family Violence*, 26, 3, 217–225.

Shalev, A.Y., Yehuda, R. and McFarlane, A.C. (Eds) (2000). *International Handbook of Human Response to Trauma*. New York: Kluwer Academic/ Plenum Publishers.

Stein, H.F. (2012/2018). 'A Mosaic of Transmissions after Trauma.' In G. Fromm (Ed.) *Lost in Transmission: Studies of Trauma across Generations*. Abingdon: Routledge.

Sule, E., Sutton, R.M., Jones, D., Moore, R., Igbo, I. and Jones, L.A. (2017). 'The past does matter: A nursing perspective on post traumatic slave syndrome (PTSS).' *Journal of Racial and Ethnic Health Disparities*, 4, 5, 779–783.

The Alliance for Intergenerational Resilience (n.d.) Accessed on 05/03/2020 at https://intergenresil.com

Van der Kolk, B.A. (2003). *Psychological Trauma*. Washington, DC: American Psychiatric Publishing.

Wilkins, E.J., Whiting, J.B., Watson, M.F., Russon, J.M. and Moncrief, A.M. (2013). 'Residual effects of slavery: What clinicians need to know.' *Contemporary Family Therapy, 35, 1, 14–28*.

Chapter 4

Ansara, Y.G. and Berger, I. (2016). 'Cisgenderism.' *The Wiley Blackwell Encyclopedia of Gender and Sexuality Studies*. Hoboken, NJ: Wiley-Blackwell Publishing.

Ansara, Y.G. and Hegarty, P. (2014). 'Methodologies of misgendering: Recommendations for reducing cisgenderism in psychological research.' *Feminism & Psychology, 24, 2, 259–270*.

Barker, M.J. and Iantaffi, A. (2015). 'Social Models of Disability and Sexual Distress.' In H. Spandler, J. Anderson and B. Sapey (Eds) *Madness, Distress and the Politics of Disablement*. Cambridge: Policy Press.

Berne, P. (2008). 'Disability, Dancing, and Claiming Beauty.' In R. Solinger, M. Fox and K. Irani (Eds) *Telling Stories to Change the World: Global Voices on the Power of Narrative to Build Community and Make Social Justice Claims*. New York: Routledge.

Calogero, R.M., Tantleff-Dunn, S.E. and Thompson, J. (2011). *Self-Objectification in Women: Causes, Consequences, and Counteractions*. Washington, DC: American Psychological Association.

CDC (Centers for Disease Control and Prevention) (n.d.a) Preventing intimate partner violence. Accessed on 04/03/2020 at www.cdc.gov/violenceprevention/intimatepartnerviolence/fastfact.html

CDC (Centers for Disease Control and Prevention) (n.d.b) Adverse Childhood Experiences (ACEs): Preventing adult trauma to improve childhood health. CDC VitalSigns. Last updated November 2019. Accessed on 05/03/2020 at www.cdc.gov/vitalsigns/aces/index.html

Coleman, E., Elders, J., Satcher, D., Shindel, A. *et al.* (2013). 'Summit on medical school education in sexual health: Report of an expert consultation.' *The Journal of Sexual Medicine, 10, 4, 924–938*.

Ellis, B.J. (1992). 'The evolution of sexual attraction: Evaluative mechanisms in women.' In J.H. Barkow, L. Cosmides and J. Tooby (Eds) *The Adapted Mind: Evolutionary Psychology and the Generation of Culture*, 267–288.

Esmail, S., Darry, K., Walter, A. and Knupp, H. (2010). 'Attitudes and perceptions towards disability and sexuality.' *Disability Rehabilitation, 32*, 14, 1148–1155.

Fredrickson, B.L. and Roberts, T.A. (1997). 'Objectification theory: Toward understanding women's lived experiences and mental health risks.' *Psychology of Women Quarterly, 21*, 2, 173–206.

Gray, J. (2011). *Mars and Venus in the Bedroom: A Guide to Lasting Romance and Passion*. London: Random House.

Haboubi, N.H.J. and Lincoln, N. (2003). 'Views of health professionals on discussing sexual issues with patients.' *Disability Rehabilitation, 25*, 6, 291–296.

Iantaffi, A. (2009). 'Disability and Polyamory: Exploring the Edges of Interdependence, Gender and Queer Issues in Non-Monogamous Relationships.' In M. Barker and D. Langdridge (Eds) *Understanding Non-Monogamies*. New York: Routledge.

Iantaffi, A. (2015). 'Gender and sexual legitimacy.' *Current Sexual Health Reports, 7*, 2, 103–107.

Iantaffi, A. and Barker, M.J. (2018). *How to Understand Your Gender: A Practical Guide for Exploring Who You Are*. London: Jessica Kingsley Publishers.

Iantaffi, A. and Mize, S. (2015). 'Disability.' In C. Richards and M. Baker (Eds) *The Palgrave Handbook of the Psychology of Sexuality and Gender*. London: Palgrave Macmillan.

Kosciw, J.G., Greytak, E.A., Zongrone, A.D., Clark, C.M. and Truong, N.L. (2018). *The 2017 National School Climate Survey: The Experiences of Lesbian, Gay, Bisexual, Transgender, and Queer Youth in Our Nation's Schools*. Gay, Lesbian and Straight Education Network (GLSEN).

Kvam, M.H. (2004). 'Sexual abuse of deaf children: A retrospective analysis of the prevalence and characteristics of childhood sexual abuse among deaf adults in Norway.' *Child Abuse & Neglect, 28*, 3, 241–251.

Lee, C. and Kwan, P.K.Y. (2014). 'The trans panic defense: Heteronormativity, and the murder of transgender women.' *Social Science Research Network.* doi:10.2139/ssrn.2430390

Love Uncommon (n.d.) Self consent: An introduction. Accessed on 10/02/2020 at https://loveuncommon.com/2017/09/28/self-consent

McDonald, K.E., Keys, C.B. and Balcazar, F.E. (2007). 'Disability, race/ ethnicity and gender: Themes of cultural oppression, acts of individual resistance.' *American Journal of Community Psychology, 39,* 1–2, 145–161.

McRuer, R. and Mollow, A. (Eds) (2012). *Sex and Disability.* Durham and London: Duke University Press.

Olsson, M. (2012). 'The digital revolution: Disability and social media.' *The McNair Scholars Journal, 11,* 179–202.

Ridgeway, C.L. and Kricheli-Katz, T. (2013). 'Intersecting cultural beliefs in social relations: Gender, race, and class binds and freedoms.' *Gender & Society, 27,* 3, 294–318.

Rojahn, J., Komelasky, K.G. and Man, M. (2008). 'Implicit attitudes and explicit ratings of romantic attraction of college students toward opposite-sex peers with physical disabilities.' *Journal of Developmental and Physical Disabilities, 20,* 4, 389–397.

Samuels, E. (2013). 'Sexy crips, or, achieving full penetration.' *Disability Studies Quarterly, 33,* 3. Accessed on 10/02/2020 at http://dsq-sds.org/article/view/3785/3248

Sexton, J.Y. (2019). *The Man They Wanted Me to Be: Toxic Masculinity and a Crisis of Our Own Making.* Berkeley, CA: Counterpoint.

Shakespeare, T., Gillespie-Sells, K. and Davies, D. (1996). *Untold Desires: The Sexual Politics of Disability.* New York: Cassell.

Stalker, K. and McArthur, K. (2012). 'Child abuse, child protection and disabled children: A review of recent research.' *Child Abuse Review, 21,* 1, 24–40.

Stewart, D.L. and Nicolazzo, Z. (2018). 'High impact of [whiteness] on trans* students in postsecondary education.' *Equity & Excellence in Education, 51,* 2, 132–145.

Sullivan, P.M., Vernon, M. and Scanlan, J.M. (1987). 'Sexual abuse of deaf youth.' *American Annals of the Deaf, 132,* 4, 256–262.

Tepper, M.S. (2000). 'Sexuality and disability: The missing discourse of pleasure.' *Sexuality and Disability, 18*, 4, 283–290

Tjaden, P.G. and Thoennes, N. (2006). *Extent, Nature, and Consequences of Rape Victimization: Findings from the National Violence Against Women Survey.* Washington, DC: US Department of Justice.

UN Women (n.d.). Facts and figures: Ending violence against women. Last updated November 2019. Accessed on 05/03/2020 at www.unwomen. org/en/what-we-do/ending-violence-against-women/facts-and-figures

University Of Michigan (2004). 'Why Men Are Attracted To Subordinate Women.' *ScienceDaily.* Accessed on 10/02/2020 at www.sciencedaily.com/ releases/2004/12/041220004026.htm

Westbrook, L. and Schilt, K. (2013). 'Doing gender, determining gender: Transgender people, gender panics, and the maintenance of the sex/ gender/sexuality system.' *Gender and Society.* doi:10.1177/0891243213503203

WHO (World Health Organization) (2013). Global and regional estimates of violence against women: Prevalence and health effects of intimate partner violence and non-partner sexual violence. Accessed on 05/03/2020 at https://apps.who.int/iris/bitstream/ handle/10665/85239/9789241564625_eng.pdf;sequence=1

Chapter 5

Altbach, P. (2003). 'American accreditation of foreign universities: Colonialism in action.' *International Higher Education, 32*, 5–7.

Bottoms, B.L., Kalder, A.K., Stevenson, M.C., Oudekerk, B.A., Wiley, T.R. and Perona, A. (2011). 'Gender differences in jurors' perceptions of infanticide involving disabled and non-disabled infant victims.' *Child Abuse & Neglect, 35*, 2, 127–141.

Cho, S., Crenshaw, K.W. and McCall, L. (2013). 'Toward a field of intersectionality studies: Theory, applications, and praxis.' *Signs: Journal of Women in Culture and Society, 38*, 4, 785–810.

Crenshaw, K. (1989). 'Demarginalizing the intersection of race and sex: A black feminist critique of antidiscrimination doctrine, feminist theory and antiracist politics.' *The University of Chicago Legal Forum*, 139.

Crenshaw, K. (1990). 'Mapping the margins: Intersectionality, identity politics, and violence against women of color.' *Stanford Law Review, 43*, 1241.

Crenshaw, K., Ocen, P. and Nanda, J. (2015). *Black Girls Matter: Pushed out, Overpoliced, and Underprotected*. Center for Intersectionality and Social Policy Studies, Columbia University. Accessed on 10/02/2020 at www.atlanticphilanthropies.org/wp-content/uploads/2015/09/BlackGirlsMatter_Report.pdf

Cusack, S. and Timmer, A.S. (2011). 'Gender stereotyping in rape cases: The CEDAW Committee's decision in Vertido v The Philippines.' *Human Rights Law Review, 11, 2,* 329–342.

Darder, A. (2017). *Reinventing Paulo Freire: A Pedagogy of Love*. New York: Routledge.

Dei, G.J.S. and Kempf, A. (Eds) (2006). *Anti-Colonialism and Education: The Politics of Resistance* (Vol. 7). Rotterdam: Sense Publishers.

Dowse, L. and Frohmader, C. (2001). *Moving Forward: Sterilisation and Reproductive Health of Women and Girls with Disabilities*, A Report on the National Project conducted by Women with Disabilities Australia (WWDA), Canberra.

Edwards, A. and Heenan, M. (1994). 'Rape trials in Victoria: Gender, socio-cultural factors and justice.' *Australian & New Zealand Journal of Criminology, 27, 3,* 213–236.

Ehrlich, S. (2003). *Representing Rape: Language and Sexual Consent*. London: Routledge.

Erevelles, N. (2014). 'Crippin'Jim Crow: Disability, Dis-Location, and the School-to-Prison Pipeline.' In L. Ben-Moshe, C. Chapman and A.C. Carey (Eds) *Disability Incarcerated*. New York: Palgrave Macmillan.

Files, J.A., Mayer, A.P., Ko, M.G., Friedrich, P. *et al.* (2017). 'Speaker introductions at internal medicine grand rounds: Forms of address reveal gender bias.' *Journal of Women's Health.' 26, 5,* 413–419.

Ford, G. (2009). 'The new Jim Crow: male and female, South and North, from cradle to grave, perception and reality: Racial disparity and bias in America's criminal justice system. *Rutgers Race & Law Review, 11,* 324.

Franklin, C.A. and Fearn, N.E. (2008). 'Gender, race, and formal court decision-making outcomes: Chivalry/paternalism, conflict theory or gender conflict?' *Journal of Criminal Justice, 36, 3,* 279–290.

Freire, P. (1996). *Pedagogy of the Oppressed (Revised)*. New York: Continuum.

Grant, J.M., Mottet, L., Tanis, J., Herman, J.L., Harrison, J. and Keisling, M. (2010). *National transgender discrimination survey report on health and health care.* Accessed on 05/03/2020 at https://cancer-network.org/wp-content/uploads/2017/02/National_Transgender_Discrimination_Survey_Report_on_health_and_health_care.pdf

Hamberg, K. (2008). 'Gender bias in medicine.' *Women's Health, 4,* 3, 237–243.

Hamberg, K., Risberg, G., Johansson, E.E. and Westman, G. (2002). 'Gender bias in physicians' management of neck pain: A study of the answers in a Swedish national examination.' *Journal of Women's Health & Gender-Based Medicine,* 11, 7, 653–666.

Hare-Mustin, R.T. (1987). 'The problem of gender in family therapy theory.' *Family Process,* 26, 1, 15–27.

Hare-Mustin, R.T. (1994). 'Discourses in the mirrored room: A postmodern analysis of therapy.' *Family Process,* 33, 1, 19–35.

Heston, T.F. and Lewis, L.M. (1992). 'Gender bias in the evaluation and management of acute nontraumatic chest pain.' *Family Practice Research Journal,* 12, 4, 383–9.

Holdcroft, A. (2007). 'Gender bias in research: How does it affect evidence based medicine?' *Journal of the Royal Society of Medicine,* 100, 1, 2–3.

Holzer, H.J., Offner, P. and Sorensen, E. (2005). 'Declining employment among young black less-educated men: The role of incarceration and child support.' *Journal of Policy Analysis and Management: The Journal of the Association for Public Policy Analysis and Management,* 24, 2, 329–350.

hooks, b. (2014). *Teaching to Transgress: Education as the Practice of Freedom.* New York: Routledge.

Howard, G., Russell, G.B., Anderson, R., Evans, G.W. *et al.* (1995). 'Role of social class in excess black stroke mortality.' *Stroke,* 26, 10, 1759–1763.

Human Rights Watch (2011). Sterilization of Women and Girls with Disabilities: A briefing paper. Accessed on 10/02/2020 at www.hrw.org/news/2011/11/10/sterilization-women-and-girls-disabilities

IFHHRO (2011). New FIGO guidelines on sterilisation of women released. Accessed on 05/03/2020 at www.ifhhro.org/news/new-figo-guidelines-on-sterilisation-of-women-released

Inter-Parliamentary Union (2018). *Women in Parliament in 2017: The Year in Review.* Geneva: IPU. Accessed on 07/02/2020 at www.ipu.org/resources/publications/reports/2018-03/women-in-parliament-in-2017-year-in-review

Jha, A.K., Varosy, P.D., Kanaya, A.M., Hunninghake, D.B. *et al.* (2003). 'Differences in medical care and disease outcomes among black and white women with heart disease.' *Circulation, 108,* 9, 1089–1094.

Jones, M. (2015) '"Suffragette" Ire Continues: Analyzing the Film's Eracism.' *Just Add Color.* Accessed on 05/03/2020 at https://colorwebmag.com/2015/10/15/suffragette-ire-continues-analyzing-the-films-eracism

Krichels, J. (2018). 'Architecture of gender.' *Oculus,* Winter edition. Accessed on 10/02/2020 at www.aiany.org/membership/oculus-magazine/article/winter-2018/architecture-of-gender

Law, V. (2011). 'Where abolition meets action: Women organizing against gender violence.' *Contemporary Justice Review, 14,* 1, 85–94.

McDowell, M.G. and Fernandez, L.A. (2018). '"Disband, Disempower, and Disarm": Amplifying the theory and practice of police abolition.' *Critical Criminology, 26,* 3, 373–391.

McLeod, A.M. (2015). 'Prison abolition and grounded justice.' *UCLA Law Review, 62,* 1156.

Moore, R. (2017). The New Jim Crow: Mass Incarceration in the Age of Colorblindness. Macat Library.

Mustard, D.B. (2001). 'Racial, ethnic, and gender disparities in sentencing: Evidence from the US federal courts.' *The Journal of Law and Economics, 44,* 1, 285–314.

National Center for Transgender Equality (n.d.). Federal Case Law on Transgender People and Discrimination. Accessed on 10/02/2020 at https://transequality.org/federal-case-law-on-transgender-people-and-discrimination

Open Society Foundations (2011). *Against Her Will: Forced and Coerced Sterilization of Women Worldwide.* Accessed on 05/03/2020 at www.opensocietyfoundations.org/publications/against-her-will-forced-and-coerced-sterilization-women-worldwide

Perley, D.G. (1993). 'Aboriginal education in Canada as internal colonialism.' *Canadian Journal of Native Education, 20,* 1, 118–28.

Pettit, B. and Western, B. (2004). 'Mass imprisonment and the life course: Race and class inequality in US incarceration.' *American Sociological Review*, 69, 2, 151–169.

Richie, B.E. (2015). 'Reimagining the movement to end gender violence: Anti-racism, prison abolition, women of color feminisms, and other radical visions of justice.' *University of Miami Race & Social Justice Law Review*, 5, 257.

Risberg, G., Johansson, E.E. and Hamberg, K. (2009). 'A theoretical model for analysing gender bias in medicine.' *International Journal for Equity in Health*, 8, 1, 28.

Rosen, J. (2013). 'The effects of political institutions on women's political representation: A comparative analysis of 168 countries from 1992 to 2010.' *Political Research Quarterly*, 66, 2, 306–321.

Rosen, J. (2018). Gender and Political Representation. Sociologists for Women in Society. Accessed on 05/03/2020 at https://socwomen.org/wp-content/uploads/2018/03/Rosen_Gender_poliRep_factsheet.pdf

Rosenberg, L., Palmer, J.R., Rao, R.S. and Adams-Campbell, L.L. (1999). 'Risk factors for coronary heart disease in African American women.' *American Journal of Epidemiology*, 150, 9, 904–909.

Sagan, E. (1988). *Freud, Women, and Morality: The Psychology of Good and Evil*. New York: Basic Books.

Samulowitz, A., Gremyr, I., Eriksson, E. and Hensing, G. (2018). '"Brave men" and "emotional women": A theory-guided literature review on gender bias in health care and gendered norms towards patients with chronic pain.' *Pain Research and Management*, 2-14. Accessed on 10/02/2020 at www.hindawi.com/journals/prm/2018/6358624

Schafran, L.H. (1989). 'Gender bias in the courts: An emerging focus for judicial reform.' *Arizona State Law Journal*, 21, 237.

Schafran, L.H. (1995). 'Credibility in the courts: Why is there a gender gap?' *Judges' Journal*, 34, 5.

Schuster, M.A., Reisner, S.L. and Onorato, S.E. (2016). 'Beyond bathrooms—meeting the health needs of transgender people.' *New England Journal of Medicine*, 375, 2, 101–103.

Sinclair, S.L. (2007). 'Back in the mirrored room: The enduring relevance of discursive practice.' *Journal of Family Therapy*, 29, 2, 147–168.

Stanley, E.A. and Spade, D. (2012). 'Queering prison abolition, now?' *American Quarterly*, 64, 1, 115–127.

Tofler, G.H., Stone, P.H., Muller, J.E., Willich, S.N. *et al.* (1987). 'Effects of gender and race on prognosis after myocardial infarction: Adverse prognosis for women, particularly black women.' *Journal of the American College of Cardiology*, 9, 3, 473–482.

Chapter 6

Adams, K. (1990/2009). *Journal to the Self.* New York: Grand Central Publishing.

Adler, J. (2002). *Offering from the Conscious Body: The Discipline of Authentic Movement.* Rochester, VT: Rochester.

Aizura, A.Z. (Ed.) (2014). *Decolonizing the Transgender Imaginary.* Durham, NC: Duke University Press.

Archer, M.S. (Ed.) (2009). *Conversations about Reflexivity.* Abingdon: Routledge.

Barker, M.J. and Iantaffi, A. (2019). *Life Isn't Binary.* London: Jessica Kingsley Publishers.

Barker, M.J. (2019). *Gender: A Graphic Guide.* London: Icon Books.

Batchelor, M. and Batchelor, S. (2001). *Meditation for Life.* Somerville, MA: Wisdom Publications.

Berila, B. (2016). *Integrating Mindfulness into Anti-Oppression Pedagogy.* New York: Routledge.

binaohan, b. (2014). *Decolonizing Trans/Gender 101.* Biyuti Publishing.

Burnard, P. and Hennessy, S. (Eds) (2006). *Reflective Practices in Arts Education* (Vol. 5). Springer Science & Business Media.

Burnham, J. (2005/2018). 'Relational Reflexivity: A Tool for Socially Constructing Therapeutic Relationships.' In C. Flaskas *et al.* (Eds) *The Space Between: Experience, Context and Process in the Therapeutic Relationship.* Abingdon: Routledge.

Cecchin, G. (1987). 'Hypothesizing, circularity, and neutrality revisited: An invitation to curiosity.' *Family Process*, 26, 4, 405–413.

Cecchin, G., Lane, G. and Ray, W.A. (1993). 'From strategizing to nonintervention: Toward irreverence in systemic practice.' *Journal of Marital and Family Therapy*, 19, 2, 125–136.

Cornell, A.W. (1996). *The Power of Focusing: A Practical Guide to Emotional Self-Healing*. Oakland, CA: New Harbinger.

Fine, C. (2010). *Delusions of Gender: The Real Science behind Sex Differences*. London: Icon Books Ltd.

Ghaye, T. (2010). 'In what ways can reflective practices enhance human flourishing?' *Reflective Practice*, 11, 1, 1–7.

Hare-Mustin, R. (1994). 'Discourses in the mirrored room: a postmodern analysis of therapy.' *Family Process*, 33, 1, 19–35.

Iantaffi, A. (2018). 'Future Directions.' In C. Richards, W. Bouman, M.J. Barker (Eds) *Genderqueer and Nonbinary Genders*. London: Palgrave.

Iantaffi, A. and Barker, M.J. (2018). *How to Understand Your Gender: A Practical Guide for Exploring Who You Are*. London: Jessica Kingsley Publishers.

Kline, N. (1999). *Time to Think: Listening to Ignite the Human Mind*. London: Ward Lock.

Neden, J. and Burnham, J. (2007). 'Using relational reflexivity as a resource in teaching family therapy.' *Journal of Family Therapy*, 29, 4, 359–363.

Oritz, N. (2018). *Sustaining Spirit: Self-Care for Social Justice*. Berkeley, CA: Reclamation Press.

Roche, J. (2019). *Trans Power: Own Your Gender*. London: Jessica Kingsley Publishers.

Stanley, L. and Wise, S. (1983/2002). *Breaking Out Again: Feminist Ontology and Epistemology*, 2nd edn. London: Routledge.

Wilson, W.A. and Bird, M.Y. (2012). *For Indigenous Minds Only: A Decolonization Handbook*. Sante Fe, NM: School for Advanced Research Press.

Index